Discovering Hope

Sharing the Journey of Healing After Miscarriage, Stillbirth or Infant Death

By Anna Sklar

Discovering Hope
© 2013 by Anna Sklar. All rights reserved.

No part of this book may be reproduced in any written, electronic, recording, or photocopying without written permission of the publisher or author. The exception would be in the case of brief quotations embodied in the critical articles or reviews and pages where permission is specifically granted by the publisher or author.

Although every precaution has been taken to verify the accuracy of the information contained herein, the author and publisher assume no responsibility for any errors or omissions. No liability is assumed for damages that may result from the use of information contained within.

All scripture quotations are from the "NIV" Bible - the HOLY BIBLE, NEW INTERNATIONAL VERSION®. NIV®.
Copyright ©1973, 1978, 1984 by International Bible Society.
Used by permission of Zondervan. All rights reserved.

Books may be purchased online:
Createspace.com
Amazon sites

Or by contacting the author at:

Anna Sklar
Email - discoveringhope@yahoo.ca
Facebook - http://facebook.com/discoveringhopeannasklar
Blog – *Living in the Moments* – http://annasklar.wordpress.com

ISBN: 978-1493740239

First Edition

*Proceeds from the sale
of this book will be used for
charity donations,
distribution of free copies,
or family mission trips.
Thank you for your support.*

To My Sons – Josiah, Caleb and Elijah
You have all blessed my heart in surprising ways.
My three most precious, unexpected gifts from God.
May each one of you be all that God intends
as He works out His plans
for your good and your future.
Jeremiah 29:11

CALEB

Faithfulness

I have set the Lord
always before me;
because He is at my right hand,
I shall not be shaken.
Psalm 16:8 (ESV)

CONTENTS

PART 1: Caleb's Story   **13**
- ❖ Pregnancy   15
- ❖ Something is Wrong   21
- ❖ Labour and Delivery   31
- ❖ Memorial Service   35
- ❖ A Grandmother's Story   41
- ❖ A Hard Choice   45

PART 2: Our Journey of Healing   **49**
- ❖ Grieving   53
- ❖ Marriage – Pulling Together or Tearing Apart?   57
- ❖ Josiah & Elijah – Caleb's Brothers   59
- ❖ Heading North & Starting Fresh   65
- ❖ Pregnant Again?   73
- ❖ Ten Years on the Journey   85

PART 3: Your Journey of Healing   **105**
- ❖ Help Me!   106
  - Your Support Network   107
  - Fellow Travelers on the Journey   109
  - Practical Ideas   135
  - *The Hospital*   135
  - *Your Child's Memorial Service*   137
  - *Remembering Your Child at Special Occasions*   139
  - *Honouring the Life of Your Child*   141

- ❖ Finding Peace   143
  - Heaven   145
  - The Bridge to Heaven   149
- ❖ There is Hope   153
  - What About My Plans?   155
  - What About My Faith?   159

PART 4: Words for the Journey   **169**
- ❖ Farewell for Now   171
- ❖ Scripture to Comfort You   174
- ❖ Books to Help You Heal   176
- ❖ Websites & Organizations for You to Visit   180
- ❖ Music to Soothe Your Soul   182
- ❖ Poems to Touch Your Heart   183

❦ INTRODUCTION ❦

We wait with hope
And we ache with hope
We hold on with hope
We let go with hope
   ❖ *With Hope,* Steven Curtis Chapman

Going back to that place, to that day in my memory, is never an easy thing to do. It is full of tragedy, sadness, pain and loss. It is a horrible day.

Once in a while I catch myself revisiting the scene, wishing it weren't a part of me, wishing my life didn't include something like that. But that day is a part of my life, a part of me, and it's a part of what makes me who I am today.

I'm talking about the day we found out our second son had died. Thirty-seven weeks in utero and suddenly gone. Big, strong, healthy and active up to that point, then still and quiet - he wasn't with us anymore.

Our hopes and dreams for him were shattered, and the grief and missing him began immediately. My heart broke in a million pieces - one huge piece would always be gone, waiting, longing for a presence that would never be a part of my life - not this life anyways.

Caleb Joshua Freedom Sklar was born on May 21, 2003. There were no newborn cries or flashes of cameras, just silence and such a heavy sadness in the room. There were no baby gifts, just tears. There were no congratulations, just "I'm so sorry." There were no last-minute preparations for bringing the baby home, just the knowledge there was so much letting go to do.

Underneath it all there was this deep, indescribable bond of love for my child. Though I wasn't going to meet him, I was still going to love him. Over time I began to understand what that meant for me - to love and be a mother to a child who had died. I am still trying to figure out how to do that, and what that looks like.

I found the first year was the hardest, but after the one-year milestone the grief seemed to lift at a greater pace, and it became easier to see beyond the present, to look more clearly to a brighter future.

This book was written as a way to walk beside you on the journey for a time. I want to share our story with you and bring you whatever encouragement and support I can for the days ahead.

I'll give you a glimpse of our grief, and show you the help, peace and hope we found as we journeyed toward healing. I'll share with you some of the journal entries, poems, articles, and blog posts I've written about our journey. I gathered together a few stories and poems from fellow travelers - they would also love to walk and talk with you for a while.

And I offer you suggestions of music, books, websites and organizations that may help you along the way.

I will be praying for you, and for your journey toward healing.

❖ *Anna Sklar*

March 8, 2007

My Tiny Man:

I have to grab hold of what God has for you and His plans. Often times they are not the same plans I have. I miss you so much today - it's the time of year - spring has brought two babies to my heart and it is almost spring.

I remember the **waiting**, and I still wait for you, dear Caleb - in this life I will always be waiting. For whatever reasons you are not here with me - your life is not what I hoped and planned. I need to open myself up to what God has for you and I know He's nowhere near done with you here on this earth - simply because we are still here - me, your daddy, your brothers and all the people who love you - you still live in our hearts.

This morning I realized that I long to help Josiah and Elijah be all that God created them to be - the same **must** be true for you, Caleb. Or I will fail you, myself and the God who made you. Gran and I were talking about this yesterday - why was your life here so short? Why did you have such little time here? And yet your impact could be the biggest one of all.

You live in **heaven**, my sweet angel, paradise - you only touched this world for an instant and all from the safety of my womb. At least you tasted chocolate! Sometimes I ponder on all you missed, yet I know you live in a world full of things beyond my comprehension - things I am missing out on for now. I just love you, I just miss you and the ache will never leave, but it will help to open myself up to God's plans for you and see where He leads.

It starts with telling your story. I pray that those who need to know about you will know about you. Let's bring hope, let's bring healing, let's bring love to broken hearts. Let's see what God made you to be. Together, my tiniest one. May God lead me and give me each word. May we reach whom He wants us to reach. May His purposes be fulfilled.

I love you with all I am and I give all to God and release you and me from my hopes and plans (once again).

For His glory and His kingdom. Always.

Mommy

Part 1
Caleb's Story

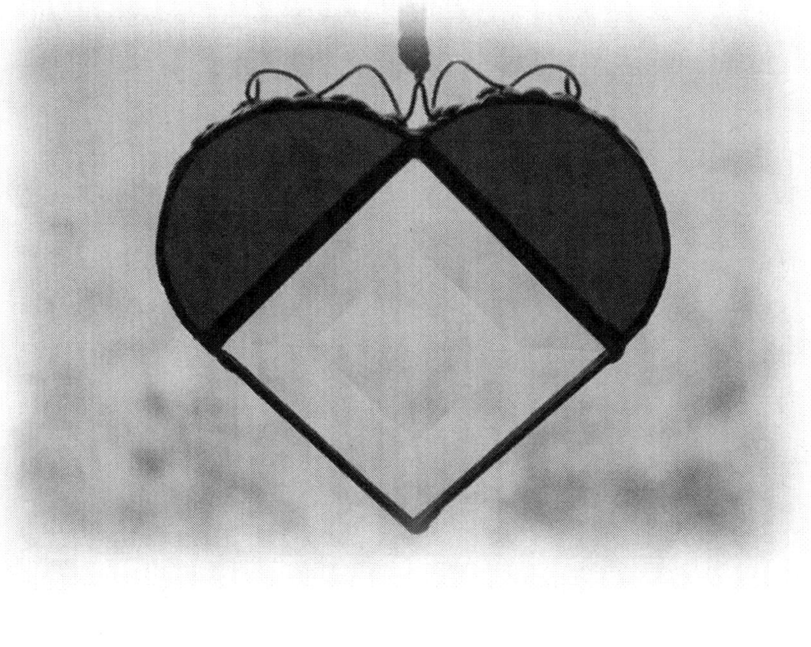

CHAPTER 1
PREGNANCY

January 30, 2003

Hello Little One!

This is the first time I write to you, though I have already talked to you **many** times and prayed for you and felt you move around inside my tummy. I feel as though I've been gradually getting to know you as you gradually grow inside of me. Every day you are becoming more and more the person God sees you to be, the person He made you to be, even though you are not yet born.

Your daddy and I are very excited that you are now a part of our little family. Your big brother Josiah can't understand yet what is happening, or that he will be a big brother soon, but we are sure he will love having you around, playing with you and loving you. We love you already, you are 22 weeks old inside my tummy - still 18 weeks left until we meet you - we can't wait to hold you and look at you and start life with you. But we know you have to stay in my tummy as long as you can so you grow big and healthy and ready to enter the world.

We saw you a couple of weeks ago (on January 13th) when mommy had an ultrasound. The doctors say you are healthy and growing normally and you look great! We got a picture of you sucking your thumb - already! You are about 6 or 7 inches long right now. When you kick inside my tummy you feel bigger than that! Your heartbeat is very strong too.

Your daddy and I and Josiah are very blessed to have you joining the family. We felt like something (or someone) was missing and we knew it was time for another baby. Mommy got pregnant right after we decided to have another baby and you've been growing inside me ever since!

You seem to be awake the most at night and love to kick inside mommy as I try to sleep. You also like to kick Josiah when he's sitting on my lap, resting up against you. You are already trying to communicate with him! I know he will love you as soon as he meets you and I know you will love him.

I'll tell you more about us next time, I'm so tired and must sleep. I just wanted to say hello and we love you so much already and feel truly blessed that you are coming into our lives. We thank God we will be the ones to love you and care for you and raise you in His plan for your life. Grow healthy and strong, little one. You are kicking right now! Saying hello back to me! I will sleep now, or at least try! I love you!

Mommy

xoxox

March 16, 2003

Hi Little Caleb:

We are visiting friends right now. We are having a wonderful, relaxing time. You have been kicking around inside me **a lot** here - I think you like being with friends!

We found out that you are a boy at mommy's second ultrasound (on February 13th) - they couldn't tell at the first one.

We are so very excited to know more about you - your name is Caleb Joshua Freedom Sklar. Your daddy really wanted to have "Freedom" in your name because we feel so free in God's will and plan for our little family.

You are almost 30 weeks old now inside mommy's tummy and getting bigger all the time! The doctors tell me you are healthy and **very** active - but I already knew that! You love to kick and roll around inside me. I can feel your little elbows and knees now. I love to connect with you that way. Mommy's biggest craving has been chocolate - especially Smarties!!

You are scheduled to arrive in the world about the second or third week of May - just two more months! We can't wait! Mommy is going to have an operation on her tummy so they can bring you into the world - just like with your brother Josiah.

Josiah likes to see mommy's "Baby" and he gives you kisses sometimes - he kisses my tummy. Although it may be different for him and he may have to get used to having you around - I know you two will love each other very much and I hope you will always be good friends.

There are many changes coming into our lives soon - we will probably be moving and daddy may start a new job - we don't know yet. God will show us as we need to know. For now we are getting ready for your arrival - in our home and in our hearts.

I love your daddy very much - he is a very good man and he loves God the most of anyone. He always asks God what we should do next and listens for the answer. He is a very caring man who already loves you very much. He is big and strong and will always protect you the best he can. He will be your best friend if you let him. He has always wanted to be a daddy and is so happy to have you and your brother Josiah. Josiah has taught him a lot about being a daddy and has taught me a lot about being a mommy. Because of your brother we are more ready for you and more relaxed about you.

I love your brother very much. He is full of energy and loves to play. He is very curious and is always exploring the world around him. He is very friendly and very loving - I'm sure he will help you a lot through life. He is just learning to talk and knows a lot of words. We are sure he'll be a good big brother to you.

I must go now, little one. Please know we are so happy you are on your way and we will always love you the best we can and we will always pray for wisdom in being your parents.

Love you,

Mommy

May 13, 2003

Dearest Little Caleb:

Last week the doctor told me the day you should arrive in the world - MAY 29th - at 1pm. Mommy has to have the operation on her tummy so you can come out, that's why we know EXACTLY when you should arrive. Sometimes mommy thinks you will come before that because I have contractions once in a while. But I hope you will wait until you are ALL READY, big and strong and healthy. Mommy has her hospital bag packed, just in case you arrive early.

 We have been rearranging our home to get ready for you and we think we are done now! And we have been getting our hearts ready to welcome you into our family. We pray for you and daddy sings to you and I rub my tummy so you can feel me touching you! Josiah still kisses my tummy and he is learning to say your name. He's been practicing swinging your baby swing too. I think he's going to love you!

 We are all very excited about you! I can't wait to hold you in my arms and touch your tiny cheeks and look into your sleepy eyes and feel your fingers wrap around mine as you sleep. Hurry little one and join us!

 We are still waiting to see where daddy will get his next job and where we will move. We hope to move a few weeks after you are born.

 All of our family and friends are very excited to meet you as well and they always ask me how you are doing. There will be so many people to love you once you arrive - they are all good people with good hearts. I will always pray that you know the person who loves you most - Jesus. And I pray He will be your best friend all your life and that God will work out His best plan for you and you will live in that plan every day of your life – there is no other way.

Mommy must sleep now little Caleb.

I love you so much,

Mommy

xoxox

CHAPTER 2

SOMETHING IS WRONG

There is no despair so absolute as that which comes with the first moments of our first great sorrow, when we have not yet known what it is to have suffered and be healed, to have despaired and have recovered hope.
❖ *George Eliot*

I opened my eyes to a new day on May 17, 2003. The sun was shining its warmth through the big bedroom window of the old house. I felt a touch of God's peace, a touch of His grace, a touch of His love in the warmth. I would need these more than ever in the days ahead.

I was thirty-eight weeks pregnant with our second son, Caleb. He was scheduled to be delivered by c-section in twelve days. Twelve days from holding another baby boy. Twelve days from Josiah meeting his little brother. The tiny nursery in the corner of our bedroom was ready. A friend was loaning me her bassinet. A baby swing stood by the bed, ready for Josiah, our 21-month-old son, to push his brother back and forth – he'd been practicing and he was ready. A change pad sat on top of our long dresser, under the window, with the Hickory Dickory Dock drawstring toy hanging overhead. We used to pull the string and sing the tune to Josiah when he was born. The music seemed to calm him.

I looked around the room that morning, looked at our lives in limbo, waiting for our visitor to cross the threshold from womb to world and become a more visible part of our family.

As the day became more real and slumber faded away, there was a jolt in my spirit, a catch in my heart. Panic.

Something is wrong.

The baby.

Caleb.

Something is wrong.

My mind raced through the last few days. His movements had slowed. The doctor said that was normal. His heartbeat was strong. She said to check his movements every couple of hours.

Then yesterday... *Yes, he's still moving. It's OK Caleb, Mommy's here. You're almost with us. Keep growing big and strong. You're almost ready!*

And this morning... *No movement. I feel different. I need to go to the clinic. Something is very wrong.*

Josh lay beside me. I didn't wake him. Maybe it was because he had come home in the middle of the night from a job interview in Seattle. Maybe it was because if I said anything to him it would be too real. I wasn't ready to make anything real. Not unless I had to.

Josiah woke up soon after me and I got him dressed and grabbed a quick breakfast for him. I decided to take Josiah with me to the clinic. I needed him there. I needed him to sit on what was left of my lap and talk to me and play with me while we waited for the doctor. We headed out the door of our apartment and into Old Reliable - our blue Pontiac Tempest.

Josiah chatted away in his car seat as I drove, and I prayed. I'm not sure what I prayed, not sure there were any real words formed in my mind. I just let my heart touch God's heart and asked Him to let everything be alright. I still hadn't felt the baby move that day and my body felt very strange.

Josiah and I waited for a little while at the clinic, but not too long. They seemed to hurry me along in the line-up. I don't know if that was because Josiah was restless or I looked panicked. Either way, the doctor had me lie down on the examination table while Josiah played on the chair.

The doctor pressed his stethoscope to my belly and listened... and listened... and listened. I kept holding my breath, waiting for him to tell me, 'Ah! There's the heartbeat! He must have been turned around all funny and was hiding that healthy, strong beat from us." But those weren't the words he finally said. What he said was, "I can't seem to find a heartbeat. But don't worry! My equipment isn't the greatest. I suggest you go straight to the hospital and make sure everything is alright."

Shock set in immediately. I went numb, didn't feel a thing. I just walked Josiah out of the clinic, drove home and handed our son over to Josh, who was now wide awake and worried.

We prayed, I hugged them, Josh must have known from my expression and my frozen emotional state that this could get very bad. We hoped for the best and decided I should go alone to the hospital because we didn't want to take Josiah into the middle of it all. It was heart-breaking to go alone, but I knew God was with me always.

On the way to the hospital I thought about the baby inside me. Our Caleb. Caleb Joshua Freedom Sklar. Quite a name, but it seemed to fit in our hearts. Caleb and Joshua were Israelite men from the Bible. They were two of twelve spies who were sent ahead into the promised land. When they brought their reports back to the people, ten men told of giants who lived in the land, giants that were too powerful to conquer. They discouraged the people from moving ahead with the plans God had, from claiming the promises God made to give His people a land "flowing with milk and honey." But two men, Caleb and Joshua, returned to the people with words of hope and confidence. Caleb encouraged the Israelites and said, "We should go up and take possession of the land, for we can certainly do it." (Numbers 13:30)

My husband's name is Joshua, so I always thought it seemed right to name our son Caleb. Josh really liked the name Josiah, so that became our older son's name, with the agreement that if any more boys followed, Caleb was the next name in line. And the Freedom in his name? Josh is part Scottish (remember Braveheart?) and wanted something a bit more contemporary in our second son's name. So Caleb Joshua Freedom Sklar it was.

We had been preparing our hearts and our home for Caleb for almost nine months. He had his own drawer full of cute baby boy clothes. Josiah had been practicing swinging the baby swing. Josh had been moving furniture and picking up baby items from people who were loaning or giving us all we needed to bring Caleb home. It was almost time. Just a few more days. What could possibly go wrong?

Yet for the last week or so I'd felt Caleb slow down so much. At my doctor's appointment that week his heartbeat had been strong. The doctor saw no need to worry and told me to count his movements every so often. I did that and Caleb seemed OK, but something in my heart was very afraid. As I drove to the hospital that fear grew and grew and I tried to give it all over to God. I pleaded with Him; I reminded Him what a good job we were doing with Josiah, I let Him know I had lots of love to give to Caleb and was very excited about him joining our family so very soon. I was so pregnant in my body, my heart, my mind, my soul. I was so full of anticipation.

Please God make this all OK.

The hospital directed me to the maternity ward and they took me right in to check the baby. Again I lay on an examination table, this time surrounded by nurses, and machines, and curtains, and hospital beds. They hooked me up to a machine that monitors the heartbeats of babies and they listened... and listened... and listened. They gave me a drink of juice and listened some more. I knew this was all going very badly and our situation was going from worse to traumatic very quickly. The nurses would glance at me, then look away, not wanting to meet my eyes, hoping for something to break the silence of the listening, willing Caleb to show us he was fine, wondering how to tell me if he wasn't. They laid their hands on my arms to show me they were with me in this. They went to get a doctor and get some answers. I still hoped. I hoped the clinic doctor was wrong, and these machines were wrong. I hoped the hospital staff were all morons who didn't have a clue how to do their job and my Caleb was just fine in all this.

The doctor came and examined me and his face said it all. I went number still. My heart was cold, just like the cold hospital room and the cold machines around me. I don't remember his words at all. I remember he sent me for an ultrasound to be absolutely sure. I remember someone wheeling me down to the ultrasound lab, then waiting in the hall, then seeing Caleb, so big on the screen, so still in black and white. Gone. I remember the ultrasound technician saying sorry, then leaving me alone for a few minutes, letting me take my time to get dressed.

I stood up from the ultrasound table, I got dressed slowly, and I closed my eyes. Something from deep within me said firmly, 'I will not be shaken' (Psalm 16:8). Already I was making the choice to hold fast to God, to my faith, to all I knew to be true. I didn't understand even a tiny part of this road I was now walking, this journey of grief I'd just embarked upon, but I still knew God was with me always.

After the ultrasound, I remember a wonderful nurse who took me into an empty room and held me while I cried.

She told me we are all given no more than we can handle and that I was going to be OK one day. I remember calling Josh from a private spot in the nurse's station, telling the man I love that his son had died before ever meeting him. I remember I couldn't get home fast enough to hold him and Josiah. I remember walking down our driveway, watching Josh run to meet me, and me saying over and over "I'm so sorry". Josh immediately alleviated any thoughts I had that this was my fault, though I'd have to learn that for myself in time.

A little while later we began the calls to our family and friends. There were so many tears and shock and questions that we couldn't answer. We just wanted them to come be with us, and they did that as soon as humanly possible.

Josh and I went for a walk by the river and left Josiah in the good care of family members. We sat down on the green grass of spring together and tried to decide what to do next. New life was everywhere, all around us, yet the one new life we looked forward to most that spring had not blossomed the way it should, had not grown the way it was supposed to, and our Caleb's life was over before it truly began. We cried together, we held each other, the sunshine reflecting on our faces from above and from the clear water beside us. So peaceful. A calm in the storm. A moment of refuge together in the eye of the hurricane. A time alone with each other, with God, and with Caleb. We gathered strength for what was to come. It had been the worst day of our lives, and the next days were going to be harder before they got easier again.

Back at the apartment, I looked around the room – my bag was packed, my husband was ready, and my son was playing with his Grandad. It was time to go. I didn't want to go to the hospital and face what I knew was coming. I had emptied my bag of all the things I wouldn't need anymore. The diapers and baby clothes were lying on the dresser now, instead of coming with me. *This is all so wrong.*

We drove to the hospital in silence, holding hands, clinging to each other in our confusion. When Josh and I arrived at the hospital we were given the room that was farthest away from the noise of the delivery ward and the nursery. I wouldn't go anywhere near the nursery during my hospital stay, but Josh stopped in there a few times during the few days we were there. I knew exactly where he'd been when he came into our room with tears in his eyes. Already we were grieving in different ways. Although I didn't understand what he was doing, I did understand that it seemed to help him.

The nurses hung a red and white, heart-shaped sun catcher outside our room - a signal to the staff that our baby had died, that our circumstances were different than those of the other filled rooms on the delivery ward, and that we needed special care and concern from them.

I remember a few nurses who stopped in just to check on us, to share similar stories, and even to share faith with us - to let us know they were praying for us and that our tiny Caleb was already in a wonderful place beyond this world. I appreciated their words, and the words did help.

I read this journal entry at Caleb's funeral...

May 20, 2003

Dearest Caleb Joshua Freedom Sklar:

Today you will be born and today we will say goodbye to you. You have already gone to be with God - I'm not sure when you went home — some time in the last few days. I don't know what happened - maybe we will find that out today too. We are so sad that you have gone, Caleb. We wanted to share our lives with you and watch you grow and love you with our whole hearts. You are our son and always will be. You will always live in our hearts. We will have to wait a little longer to meet you. God is holding you in His big strong hands and Jesus smiles on your beautiful, precious, tiny face. You hear the angels singing. You are whole before you were ever born. You will never see this world or the beauty that abounds in it. But the only world you will know is the most beautiful because it is God's home.

I don't know if I have the strength to say goodbye to you without ever looking in your eyes or feeling your tiny fingers wrap around mine. God gives us strength for the day. There will be some family here to say goodbye as well.

When they told me yesterday that you had died, when they couldn't find your heartbeat, my whole world changed. It is a much emptier place without you and there will always be a hole where you should have been. Your daddy is so sad, we have both cried so many tears, and there are more to come. Please know we loved you from the start and we wanted you to be part of our little family.

We will tell Josiah about you one day, when he is old enough. And he will be sad too. We place you in God's hands, little one, and look forward to the day we will meet you in your heavenly home.

Blessings on you angel boy, I love you,

Mommy

xoxox

~ CHAPTER 3 ~
LABOUR AND DELIVERY

Each life, no matter how fragile or brief... forever changes the world.
❖ *Author Unknown*

I don't remember much about the next 24 hours - the epidural makes things a little fuzzy for me. We had to choose how to deliver Caleb. I was scheduled to have a c-section with him the following week, but the doctor recommended that I try to deliver him naturally instead. I remember being induced at 9 a.m., waiting through a long labor, being ready to push just after midnight, and delivering Caleb at 2:45 a.m.

There were no answers when Caleb was born. He appeared healthy, big and strong. The doctors asked if we wanted an autopsy to try and discover more about the reasons for his death, but we just chose not to do that. The placenta was later tested for Group B Strep and the test came back positive. That means that infection is a possibility, but not a certainty. I had too much amniotic fluid for a while during pregnancy, but then the fluid levels seemed to balance on their own. That may have something to do with his death. Caleb's heartbeat was strong just a few days before he died, so there were no real conclusions, only guesses.

I do remember holding him – he was so still and he looked so serious. I kept willing him to open his eyes, to move even the slightest bit, to let everyone know they were wrong about him. But his dark curly locks remained so still, and his button nose never twitched. I knew he was gone. I knew it the moment I'd woken up two days earlier, but I wished with all my heart that he would be with us.

Caleb stayed in our room with us for a few hours after he was born. I watched as a few others held him - for some it was too hard and that was OK with us. I tried to absorb everything I could about him before I had to say goodbye. The hospital let him lie in a bassinet in the room with us for the rest of the night. We were exhausted, but we didn't sleep much, we didn't want this one precious night together to end. Our only night with him - it was so bittersweet. I would try to sleep, then wake up suddenly and reach for him, knowing it would be time to say goodbye very soon.

We snapped a few pictures and soaked up all we could about him - he looked just like his big brother, he had Josh's toes, and the Collier cleft chin (from my side of the family). He was a big boy (8lbs 1oz.), and looked very strong and serious. We caught just a glimpse of him as he was on this earth.

As dawn arrived, we knew our time with Caleb was getting shorter. The people from the funeral home arrived about 9 a.m. One of the hardest things we had to do was place Caleb in the arms of the wonderful woman who helped us through all the "arrangements" of the next couple of days. I remember feeling such deep sorrow as I gently placed my newborn son in her arms. I was overwhelmed by confusion, but I was also overwhelmed with love for Caleb. We physically gave him over that day, but then we had to start the long process of handing him over in a spiritual and emotional sense.

That was May 21, 2003. As Caleb had already arrived at the final destination of his journey - his heavenly home - so now we began our journey of grief and healing as a family, together with our oldest son, Josiah David.

May 21, 2003

WHAT WE SEE

Ask me what I see...
I see my home in heaven.
I see angels singing, angels dancing.
I see golden streets and glorious mansions.
I see rooms prepared for me and you.
But most of all, I see Jesus welcoming me home,
feel His arms around me,
and I am safe as I wait for you...

Ask us what we see...
We see our beautiful boy at home in heaven.
We see him singing and dancing with the angels.
We see him walk the golden streets with grace and ease.
We see him waiting for us to join him there.
We see him free.

❖ *Josh and Anna Sklar*

We wrote this poem together after Caleb went to the funeral home.

CHAPTER 4
MEMORIAL SERVICE

... the visitation is the social release of the body, the funeral service is the spiritual release, and the burial is the physical release.
  ❖ *Ed Vining*

Josh and I sat in what was once his office at the church. He had recently been laid off from his position as the youth pastor – due to budget cuts. The office was located off the front foyer of the church.

We held the blank bulletin in our hands. The cover reads, "Lovingly He guides our steps to Heaven's door where He greets us with the majesty of a King." And "Thine eyes shall see the King in His beauty; they shall behold the land that is very far off." (Isaiah 33:17)

What did we want to say? How could we honour Caleb best in one short memorial service?

We included an order of service. We also shared a poem about our Caleb that Josh and I had written after the birth, after we handed Caleb over, while I was recovering in the hospital room for one day following the delivery. And we thanked people for coming to honour our tiny boy, and we let them know we chose to hold on to hope.

We asked a good friend and mentor to perform the service. His words that day were comforting to our hearts, it was good to hear his voice give a message to those in attendance about our Caleb and the Caleb of the Bible. We asked a wonderful lady to sing *His Eye is on the Sparrow* in her beautiful way and she filled our hearts to overflowing and the tears flowed freely for all that day. I read a journal entry I'd written to Caleb just before I was induced in the hospital. Josh carried Caleb's too-small casket in his hands. There were about 200 people there that day.

Our Josiah was there too – he was about 21 months old at the time. We couldn't imagine him not being at his brother's funeral, even though all the pamphlets I'd been given said that parents should not bring young children into situations where there will be a lot of crying, emotion, etc. Yet I couldn't imagine keeping Josiah from any of the too-few things we got to do as a family. So we chose to bring him with us, to include him, to let him be a part of the grieving and the healing, hoping it would help him to understand and heal in some way. He made people smile at the funeral, his life and laughter eased so much of the sadness and heavy feeling of death. He danced as the music played, he crawled from one person's lap to another, comforting and bringing joy as he went along his merry way, hugging each one. Family members offered to take him into the foyer if he got rowdy, but he never did. I think he needed to be there just as much as we did.

Many people were blessed at Caleb's funeral. One friend wrote this about the service: "...definitely angels all around that day... As I looked around that church I saw so many people in tears, especially women, and I'm sure there were many there who have gone through a similar experience."

I remember my mum kept trying to make me sit down after the service, but I just wanted to greet everyone. There wasn't going to be many maternal duties for me to perform in Caleb's life, and I wasn't going to miss this chance. Besides, I needed to store up the love of all these friends and family in my heart to face the long road of grief ahead. I needed to see their smiles and feel their hugs and look into their eyes and know without a doubt that that I was loved, and my Caleb was loved too.

The internment followed. White carnations were laid on the tiny casket. Caleb was buried in the same plot as his great-grandpa. This was the only way we found peace as we laid him to rest. We felt like we could, in a way, see with our eyes that he was already with others who would take very good care of him. He was not alone.

> CALEB JOSHUA FREEDOM SKLAR
>
> MAY 21, 2003
>
> Surrounded by Glory

Josiah got into the car with his grandma, his uncle and his aunt after the internment. Josh and I went back to the apartment for a couple more days of regrouping. Friends had offered us their cottage for a few days and we were going to take them up on the offer. We needed to get away and get ourselves together a bit more before returning to real life.

Two days after the funeral, we picked up Josiah from his grandma's, and we headed north to the cottage.

CALEB'S SONG

Mother? Father?
I just wanted you to know
That I'm fine... yes, so fine.
I am safe and warm in Heaven.
Jesus holds me in His arms.
His voice is song, His eyes are kind.

It seems I could not stay;
I just had to leave
To see my Heavenly Father's face.
Jesus tells me that you miss me
And your hearts are aching...
How I wish you felt His Great Embrace.

Do you know that He rocks me
Like you would do?
And His kisses are soft and sweet...
He sings in my ear
And snuggles me near,
In tenderness so complete.

I did not have the chance to learn
Just who of you was who...
I needed just a little more time.
The low voice, was that you, Dad?
I know yours, Mom, it's higher!
I would have learned it well in time.

There's so much I would say
If I only knew the words
And could make my awkward mouth
Shape the sound.
But I have not learned to speak...
Although you'd think I'd pick up some
With such a noisy family around!
I want you to know how I'm feeling.

Even though I'm in Paradise.
I miss you…
I miss you.
I will never forget you…
Thank you for my life.

Thank you for my life,
For I took so long to grow.
Thank you for your love.
He promised you would love me…
I feel how you love me…
But now I live with Him above.

I never had the chance
To say I love you,
So hear me pray it now, hear me say…
"Dear Father, Dear Mother,
And little Big Brother,
I love you,
I'll love you always."

Adele Simmons

Adele is a good friend of ours.

She gave this song to us at Caleb's funeral.

She also sang *His Eye in on the Sparrow* for us during the service.

CHAPTER 5

A GRANDMOTHER'S STORY

My mum wrote this for me in 2009…

The voice on the other end of the line was my daughter, Karen.

"Mum, Anna's baby died. Caleb died!"

The red heart hung from the doorway outside my daughter's hospital room. A sign that the baby about to be born had already died.

God give me strength.

Anna was in bed, talking, trying her best to smile and accept what was about to happen.

All I could do was wait.

I rubbed her legs as she shook with the medication she had been given.

We talked with an ever growing procession of friends and family who had come to support her and Josh and take care of Josiah.

Tried to sing hymns. Nothing would come to mind.

Feeling so useless.

Then sitting for an eternity in the waiting room.

The moment came. After wanting the wait to be over the nurse brought no relief.

I knew the worst was to come.

We walked into Anna's room.

There she was in bed, trying to look brave.

Josh by her side, sitting on the bed.

She looked so tired and so heartbroken.

In her arms she held her newborn son.

"Mum, this is our new baby boy, Caleb."

It was the worst thing I have ever done.

The worst sight I have ever seen.

The saddest feeling.

The most agonizing pain.

Seeing her and Josh and Caleb.

I fought back the tears that had welled inside.

She passed him to me.

My new grandson.

A child I would never get to know here on Earth.

The times I talked to him in his mother's womb now gone.

Only emptiness and sadness remained.

I held him for the first and last time.

Stroked his tiny face.

Soaked in every moment.

Then I passed him to his other grandma.

I knew she was feeling the same pain and I grieved for her too.

I said a silent prayer that we would all get through this horrible experience.

The next few days I was numb.

There were things to do and people to call.

The day of the funeral arrived.

Anna had a long delivery and was supposed to still be in the hospital resting. Instead she was in the washroom at the church preparing to bury her son.

She put on the sweater I had brought. She didn't have any clothes that fit except maternity.

I went in to the family room to see Caleb one last time.

I knew he wasn't there, just his body.

I knew he was with the Lord in a better place but that brought little comfort right now.

He was wearing the outfit Josh had bought the day before.

Wrapped in a blanket.

I kissed his tiny face and said *Goodbye*.

There were 350 or more people there.

People who loved Anna and Josh and Josiah and had looked forward to loving Caleb too.

I knew the Lord would use our grief to bring others to Christ.

That all those people there were touched somehow by this tiny child.

They would remember when times in their lives got tough.

They would seek God's face.

Lives would be changed and Caleb's purpose fulfilled.

This tiny boy would lead them.

We prayed, we sang.

Anna and Josh both said beautiful things about their baby boy.

Adele sang *His Eye is on the Sparrow* and they played *I Can Only Imagine*.

We gathered at the grave site.

This isn't the way it's supposed to be.

I clung to a dear friend and stood by my family.

Caleb was buried with his great-granddad but we all knew that they were both already

Surrounded by Glory

I picture him walking quietly and peacefully with another man, maybe his great grandad, maybe Jesus, talking and laughing.

He's all grown up with long wavy hair and a smile that would melt everyone's heart.

Perfect and complete.

I'm grateful to God for giving me that vision.

It brings me comfort now and I look forward to the day when I will see him running up to greet me with that big smile.

I can only imagine.

❖ *Gran*

CHAPTER 6

A HARD CHOICE

"I wish it need not have happened in my time," said Frodo. "So do I," said Gandalf, "and so do all who live to see such times. But that is not for them to decide. All we have to decide is what to do with the time that is given us."
   ❖   J.R.R. Tolkien, Fellowship of the Ring

We drove north. Going all the way back to our dating days, this has been our custom. We are pulled by it somehow, like an invisible magnet has a hold on us, constantly drawing us northward. Friends of ours have a cottage in Northern Ontario, and when they offered it to us for a few days after the funeral, no discussion was needed. We packed up and drove north. Josiah was picked up from Grandma's house and off on new adventures. He was enjoying all his travels.

We slept more than usual, ate whatever was unhealthy, played with Josiah, gazed at the river, and watched TV. Josh would take Josiah for rides on the ATV and Josiah would fall asleep with the motion of the vehicle. Then Josh would carry him inside and lay him on the bed, surrounded by pillows to keep him safe. Then we would fall asleep, or read books, or gaze out the big windows. We were very quiet during those few days, deep inside ourselves, not quite sure what to make of our new normal.

I remember standing on the dock at the cottage one day, about a week or so after Caleb's death. Josh and Josiah had gone to the general store for a few groceries, and I was left to my own thoughts for a while. I wandered out to the dock and stood looking at the dark water below. The water looked just how I felt. Dark, empty, void, and unstable. I sat down on the dock, getting closer to the water, wanting to touch it. The darkness of the water looked inviting and peaceful.

It seemed that pain, sorrow, confusion and doubt might just disappear in that darkness. For a few moments I almost convinced myself that entering into the darkness would reunite me with Caleb, because he was in the darkness. I couldn't reach out to him, couldn't touch him, couldn't hold him or rock him. I just wanted to be with my baby.

Then my eyes looked to the horizon. And darkness met with light. The beautiful blues and whites in the sky above gave a wonderful contrast to the black water below.

Caleb isn't in the darkness, he's in the light. He is nowhere that is below, he is everywhere that is above. He is surrounded by love and joy, never by emptiness. If I want to be with Caleb, I must look up, never down.

This was my first experience with a desperate longing for heaven. Since that day I have noticed an unquenchable thirst for my heavenly home on many occasions. Most days I am getting better with the waiting.

God spoke to my heart on that dock. He asked me to keep going with the life He'd given me. He asked me to keep my eyes focused on Him, to remember all He'd given me to do in being a wife to Josh and a mother to Josiah. He reminded me of all the reasons I had to praise Him, all the blessings He'd already given me. Praise was the last thing I wanted to do, but I knew that for now, all I had to do was try to focus on what I already had in my life, instead of what I didn't have. This choice is one that I continue to make on a daily basis at times.

This poem describes those moments on the dock…

THE EDGE

I stood on the edge
The edge of my mind
The edge of my past
The edge of my future
The edge of my existence
The edge of my faith
The edge of me

I stood on the edge
I saw my son
I saw my God
I saw myself

I stood on the edge
I chose to live
I chose to love
I chose to believe
I chose to walk

Forward
One step at a time
One day at a time
One life at a time

I stood on the edge
And saw us
United
Soon
Forever
And Ever
Amen

❖ *Anna Sklar*

I envisioned myself reaching my hand out to God, walking off the dock, away from the darkness of the water, towards the light of the life He'd given me, leaving the rest with Him to sort out, not yet trusting, but just leaning on my faith to continue me on the journey, one step at a time.

Part 2
Our Journey of Healing

Late June, 2003

I want to use this book to heal now. I may write to you sometimes, all the time, I may write to God or others, I don't know just yet.

I hope you know that I love you to the depths of my being and I miss you so much it hurts. It has been almost a month now since you died, since you left this world and went to your heavenly home.

I am happy you live in paradise and walk in the presence of our Lord and sing and dance with the angels. But I do miss you so much. Your daddy has shed more tears than I have, he is so very sad sometimes and he really misses you and loves you.

There's so much to say already - where do I start? In many ways, I got to hold you for 9 months and feel you kick in my belly. I knew you the best of anyone because we spent every second together for 38 weeks. I was the only home you ever knew here in this world.

I have also realized that there were so many things I intended you to be in my life and daddy's life and your brother Josiah's life - none of these were what God intended you to be in our lives. I must open myself up to what God intended you to be and that is one of the first steps toward healing.

There were many days at the beginning, just after we lost you, that I didn't want to get better physically - I just wanted to be with you, in heaven. Then I would look at your daddy and your brother and I knew that I was still blessed, even though I'd lost you. God is still there and He is still good and I can still turn to Him and trust Him.

I've realized how little control I actually have in life. I've realized how short life is and how each minute must be enjoyed to the fullest.

I've been reminded just how precious your brother is and how important a job it is to be his mom.

I have renewed love for your daddy - deeper, stronger, fuller, more intimate love. He is just **amazing**.

And I thank God you have a wonderful home ready for you and that you have already met the Saviour. Heaven seems a lot less far away with you there. Please know I look forward to the day I will hold you in my arms in paradise. Until then I will live to the fullest and love with my whole heart and seek God's will always.

I love you Caleb.

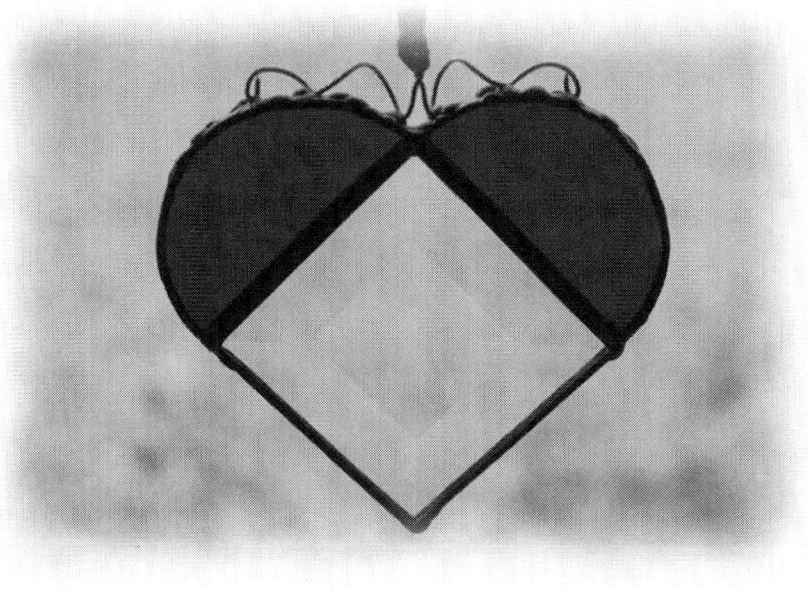

CHAPTER 7

GRIEVING

In the storms of life, sometimes God calms the storm... sometimes He calms His child.
   ❖ *Craig Groeschel*

I had never really known grief until my Caleb passed away. My life had brought sadness, regret, and hurt, but never the deep-down-in-my-bones feeling that came with grief.

At first my grief seemed all-consuming, overwhelming, almost like I was suffocating at times. I would be crying, sobbing from deep in my soul one minute, then laughing hysterically the next minute. It was such a roller-coaster ride at first, and there was such intensity in my emotions. This was new to me, I'm not usually one to cry very much. I tend to bottle my emotions up inside, or write them out into words to express them.

One thing I learned immediately was that grief looks different in each of our lives. My emotions seemed to be the complete opposite of my husband's emotions at times. I was never very angry about Caleb's death, but my husband experienced this emotion so deeply sometimes, and had many "words" with God. It was crucial to let myself grieve, feel, and heal in my own ways. Josh needed to do the same in his own ways.

A truly healing part of my journey came when I felt free to acknowledge Caleb's life instead of shoving it under the rug. When I felt free to talk about him and acknowledge that a person very dear to my heart had passed away, I found such amazing peace in that.

I think often times, because our babies came and went so quickly through this world, it is hard to realize the truth that their lives are still very significant, their impact is still very great, and our love for them is still very strong. It was so strange to me sometimes that I could feel such grief for someone I had never known very well. But I knew Caleb the best of anyone, I am his mother, and his life is very dear to my heart and always will be, no matter how short it turned out to be.

After the first few weeks my grief changed into something that seemed more manageable. I was getting through the days a little better, I was a little more focused on tasks or topics of conversation, and I was starting to see through the fog of my confusion just a little better.

From then on, my state of mind seemed to continuously improve, even if only slightly, from week to week and month to month. I found a great lifting in my spirits after passing the one-year milestone.

Still to this day there are times when I find myself in such a grumpy mood and I don't have the slightest idea what's wrong, then after a while I realize that I just really miss Caleb that day. Initially this happened around the 21st of each month, since that was the anniversary of his passing.

If you find that your grief is not improving, and that you are increasingly depressed, or that others are increasingly concerned for your well-being, please seek help through a counselor. On two occasions my husband and my mother encouraged me to talk to a counselor because they were worried about my state of mind. I didn't question their opinions, they know me best, and they arranged the appointments for me. I followed through in seeing the counselors and was reassured I was doing OK. This also eased the minds and hearts of my family - so it was good all around.

During one of my counseling sessions, I learned that grief can come in and out of our lives like waves. Sometimes the storm is raging and the waves are high, relentless, pounding at us with such heavy force. Other times the waves are calm and gentle, lapping at us with a serene comfort. Whatever you're experiencing at this moment, the storms will pass, and though they may come again, the waves will get smaller and smaller, and will subside to rolling touches on the shore, making the sand smooth to walk on.

As you journey through your grief, know that God is sharing the path with you. He knows your deepest emotions, He understands the hurt, and He wants to help you heal. He will be your faithful companion in the hours, days, weeks, months, and years ahead.

CHAPTER 8

MARRIAGE – PULLING TOGETHER OR TEARING APART

Grief and sadness knits two hearts in closer bonds than happiness can; common sufferings are far stronger than common joys.
  ❖ *Alphonse de Lamartine*

When Caleb died I remember how much Josh and I pulled together in the initial loss. Josh was amazing, strong, and even funny sometimes - he even made me laugh a little. One thing that really stands out for me is that he never blamed me. There were many times when I had to deal with these strong feelings that Caleb's death was my fault. He lived in my body so I felt responsible for his death. I would play the circumstances leading up to Caleb's stillbirth over and over in my mind, wondering what I had done wrong. Josh would reassure me every time that it was not my fault. I really needed that, I relied on that, and his words eventually came to be truth for me.

We did really well the first couple of months. Life kept us busy and we had no choice but to keep up with all that was happening. The crash came for us about two or three months after the fact. We started fighting, we were frustrated and irritable, and we started turning away from each other instead of towards each other.

This was when the hard work of rebuilding our relationship began. We were different people, the loss had changed us, and we needed to learn to be there for each other and love each other after the loss. There were different, newer aspects of our personalities to explore and reconcile in the wake of Caleb's death. He has brought out so much good in us, and with that also came some bad.

It would take months of rebuilding to get to a point where we were OK. But those months were not horrible, just hard. I'm so glad we worked through it all together and joined with each other in the journey of healing. Our relationship is much stronger because of all the growth we experienced. We didn't ask for it, or plan on it, but this was our life. Caleb's death brought a whole different dimension to our relationship. We have a deeper love for each other now, a deeper trust in God, and a deeper understanding of the hurt of others.

Eventually we were able to use our experiences to help many people on the journey. Hopefully as you are reading this we are helping you as well.

CHAPTER 9
JOSIAH & ELIJAH CALEB'S BROTHERS

When the heart grieves over what it has lost, the spirit rejoices over what it has left.
 ❖ *Sufi Epigram*

Our oldest son, Josiah, experienced his little brother's death when he was about 21 months old. Except for the few days he spent with his Grandma while we were in the hospital and arranging the funeral, he was with us 24/7 and witnessed our tears, our sadness and our hurt. I'm sure he noticed the issues of death in his own way and hurt in his own way. He would amaze me with his insight, even at such a young age.

Josiah was there at the funeral and internment. For a long time afterwards, every time we would drive by a cemetery, he would say, "Caleb?" For a few years, when we would visit his gravesite, Josiah loved to play with the pinecones that were always scattered around. He loved to decorate Caleb's stone with them and bring a few home in the car.

The hospital hung a beautiful heart-shaped sun catcher outside our room while I was delivering Caleb - a sign to all the staff that the baby delivered here would be stillborn. Then they gave us the sun catcher to take home. A few months after Caleb's death, Josiah noticed it hanging in our window and said, "Caleb" - I was amazed he would remember such a thing, and associate the two - even months later.

During the months that followed Caleb's death, Josiah would occasionally find me in my bedroom, crying, and I would tell him Mommy misses Caleb. Sometimes we'd look at his memory box - Josiah would ask 2-year-old questions and he'd hug me and kiss me - it really helped both of us in the healing process.

A bond has formed between your other children and your baby. I could already tell that our baby, Caleb, loved his big brother, Josiah, very much. Caleb would respond to Josiah's cries, his laughs, his voice, and he would constantly kick Josiah when he was sitting on my lap. And Josiah was very excited about Caleb's arrival. He used to kiss my tummy and say, "Baby". He saw all the baby equipment set up around the house, and though he was not even two years old he would go to the baby swing and push it back and forth to practice. After Caleb's death, Josiah continued to kiss my tummy and about two months afterward he came up to kiss my tummy and noticed, "Baby gone."

I've tried my best to honour the brotherly bond between Josiah and Caleb. I've tried to be open with Josiah in hopes of helping him heal, not to depress him. I tell Josiah about Caleb's beautiful home, we dream about what Caleb is seeing and doing in heaven, and we talk about what we look forward to doing with him one day (Josiah wants to wrestle his little brother and see how strong he is).

I wrote this truth in an email to a friend a few months after Caleb's death, "Josiah is growing more and more each day, and continues to be my greatest helper in healing and looking to what is ahead!"

To this day, Josiah is still very open about his heavenly brother. All of his teachers at school know about Caleb. I remember one day he mentioned Caleb to my friend at church. Josiah noticed a family with three babies and said,

"We had three babies in our family too, but one of them died."

At first this used to just floor me and I had no idea how to react, but over time I've learned to smile and agree, and move on to the next subject, even though my heart jumps down my throat every time.

Our youngest son, Elijah, was also very open about Caleb after we told him about his other older brother. He is a very different personality, doesn't ask the same questions Josiah did, and just seems to understand that Caleb lives in heaven with God.

Your other children will heal from the loss in their own ways. Their honesty may cut straight to the core of your being at times. Their questions, reflections and thoughts may make you reach deep inside yourself to find strength and love you never knew you had. Though it may always be hard to go there, to reach that far, it's worth the effort in helping every one of your family members to walk through their own journeys of healing.

August 30, 2003

Dearest Caleb:

Tonight it is hard. Tonight I miss you more than I can bear. Tonight the confusion is too much, the reality of your death too clear, the pain too sharp. Why aren't you here? Why aren't I holding you in my arms? Why aren't I hearing your giggle, watching you grow, seeing your smile? Why isn't Josiah playing with you? Why aren't you keeping him company in the car? Why didn't you watch him tonight as he danced around before his bath? Why isn't he enjoying your presence, reveling in the audience you should have been? I don't understand. I am at such a loss.

Josh shared his testimony last night at camp. I guess he talked about you. A little girl who heard the story came up to me this morning and said, "I'm sorry your son died." Such pure, honest, innocent sorrow from such a young soul. Her angel must have been standing right beside her, telling her what to say, and as she spoke the words delivered to me straight from heaven, I touched you once again for a brief second. And I miss you, Caleb. Sometimes I long for the sadness to disappear, for the ache to go away, but I know it means I truly did love you; I truly am your mommy. I just have to wait longer than I thought to meet you.

I'm going to speak to a counselor in about a week and maybe he can help me deal with my sadness a little better. I am not treating your daddy as I should - I don't know everything behind it, I suspect it is a lot of things, but my sadness over you is one, I'm sure.

I love you, angel boy. I wish so desperately that you were here, but if you can't be here than I'm so glad you are in Paradise.

See you later,

Mommy

xoxox

CALEB?

Do you hear them, Caleb?
Do you hear the angels sing?
Do you see Him, Caleb?
Do you behold the King of Kings?
Do you walk on them, Caleb?
Do you tread the streets of gold?
Do you talk to them, Caleb?
Do you converse with saints of old?
Do you bask in it, Caleb?
Do you grow in the Saviour's love?
Do you enjoy it, Caleb?
Do you like your mansion above?
Do you dance in them, Caleb?
Do you twirl in rainbow colours?
Do you know them, Caleb?
Do you love your heavenly mothers?
Do you miss me, Caleb?
Do you long for my embrace?
Do you remember me, Caleb?
Do you search for my face?
Do you wait for me, Caleb?
Do you wonder where I am?
Do you know the day is soon, Caleb?
When I'll hold your tiny hand…

❖ *Anna Sklar*

◈ CHAPTER 10 ◈
HEADING NORTH AND STARTING FRESH

If one dream should fall and break into a thousand pieces, never be afraid to pick one of those pieces up and begin again.
  ❖ *Flavia Weedn*

When we started our journey of healing there was an overwhelming sense of emptiness and confusion. We were supposed to be holding a new baby boy, welcoming him into our family, watching him grow before our eyes, and making wonderful memories with him. But there was none of that. So we were lost for a long time, and it was compounded by Josh's recent lay-off and having to move.

This is an article I wrote in 2006, describing what we were going through in the year following Caleb's death...

THE YEAR OF THE STORM

We moved to Sudbury in a snowstorm. Most of our worldly possessions were packed in a small U-Haul. We towed our '91 Pontiac Tempest behind us, stuffed with clothes and odds and ends. All the moving of the past eight months had forced us to scale down to necessities. We kept only what we needed and what we just couldn't part with. Our son, Josiah, sat in his car seat, oblivious to all the changes, all the turmoil of the year of 2003. He was happy if we were happy, our love was his home. Eight hours of slippery, slushy, snowy driving conditions allowed us plenty of time to think. The recent events of our life seemed to have passed in a dream world, like everything had happened to someone else and I was just an observer, amazed by what I saw. 'How do they carry on? Why is their marriage still intact? How can their son still be so happy? What awaits them in Sudbury?' It was hard to believe it was my own life I was pondering. We left our family and friends in southern Ontario to pursue a life full of unknowns. How would we survive? Where would Josh work? Would we meet new friends? When would our hearts heal? The only certainty we had was Sudbury was our choice, our hope, our future.

Eight months earlier Josiah was one and a half years old, we were expecting our second son, and Josh was working as a youth pastor. Life was good - busy, but good. Then our world began to change. Josh was laid off unexpectedly. He left one morning for a breakfast meeting with the church leaders, and came home stunned and confused. We thought this was just a bump in the road and that Josh would be back to work in no time. The plus side was the three months of severance pay the church provided for us. We didn't feel much stress at that point and actually enjoyed a lot of quality family time together. We spoiled ourselves as we used up our medical benefits on massages and chiropractic treatments. Josh started working out at the gym two or three hours a day, we took long walks with our son, caught up with friends and family, and went out on dates. We tried to make the most of the gift of family time as Josh searched for another job and we awaited the birth of boy number two.

Three months quickly passed and once again our world turned upside down. It was ten days before my scheduled c-section and Josh had gotten in late the night before from a job interview in Seattle. As I awoke that morning I thought something was wrong, I just felt different.

I let Josh sleep, I didn't want to share my unfounded worries, and took Josiah to the medical clinic with me. This is when time stopped for me, when the dream world began. Numerous doctors, monitors and an ultrasound confirmed my worst fears. Our second son, Caleb Joshua Freedom Sklar, had died in utero.

The next few days were full of hard decisions, tears, and grief as we delivered Caleb and laid him to rest. It is true - no one should ever have to bury a child. I remember I felt as though the world had stopped turning. Suddenly all that we thought our lives would be had changed. For three months we had searched and there was still no job for Josh, and now there was no new baby to bring home.

One interpretation of Josiah's name is "God Has Healed." How amazing it was to be with him as he lived up to his name. Every smile, hug, and kiss from him seemed more precious and we marveled at him as we grieved the loss of Caleb. Josh and I had both lost our foothold on our roles in life, yet Josiah kept us grounded. We were still his parents, we still had a job to do, and there was still reason to get up in the morning and grab all we could from the day.

Then came more hard choices. No jobs had opened up for Josh and we had to survive somehow. Where to go? What to do? What now? One opportunity remained, one door was still open. It was a temporary job, just for the summer, and it would mean giving up our apartment and putting most of our things in storage. We would work at a children's camp in northern Ontario for the summer. Josh would be the waterfront director and I would run the snack shop.

*We stuffed what we could into our old car, tied a bag of clothes and a stroller to the roof, and made the five-hour drive north to camp. We hoped the change of scenery and the new people we'd meet would be just what we needed. We were not disappointed. It was a good summer. We were busy, but we were surviving, and we managed to make some good memories as we watched Josiah blossom at the onset of his second birthday. The tiny church near the camp offered to let us stay in their parsonage for the summer. It was an old three-bedroom farmhouse on the lake - a beautiful place to grieve and reflect and find our happiness in what we **did** have. There were also more interviews for Josh, and the three of us even made a trip to Maryland, Washington for a prospective job, but still nothing panned out.*

The summer ended and we were still searching, still stunned, and still confused. We stuffed our car once again and headed back to southern Ontario for my sister's wedding. Afterwards we stayed with Josh's mom for a few weeks as we awaited the outcome of yet another prospective job. That one also fell through, and we were so discouraged. We were down to nothing. No job, no money, no prospects, no future.

We sat down and talked about the next step. We realized the only place we'd seen hope for our little family in the past eight months was in the north. We decided to cling to that, to chase after a future, to live out our hope. That's how we found ourselves buckled into a U-Haul as we headed north to Sudbury.

Now we exist in the future we were chasing, and the hope we saw. Josiah is now four and a half years old, our third son, Elijah, was born May 13th, 2005, we own our own home, and Josh is once again a pastor in the church.

The road to Sudbury was much longer than an eight-hour drive in the snow. Some of the baggage we brought was unseen, carried in our hearts, forever a part of us. We're glad we made the trip, despite the storm that brought us here.

Sudbury has been a place of healing for us. We were so broken and tired when we arrived here; God has renewed and restored us, step by step, in the ten years that we have lived here. Sudbury is a mining town and for a long time boasted the tallest smokestack in the world. Decades of mining took their toll on Sudbury, and by the 1970's the landscape here was described as similar to the moon - barren, unable to support plant life, with polluted water systems. It was a place that had been chewed up and spit out in the name of mining.

Years before we moved here we visited good friends in Sudbury, and I remember seeing nothing but black rock and dead trees as we drove into town. I had no desire to live here then! I took Environmental Studies in university, and I remember working through a case study of Sudbury because of its pollution problems. But there was hope for this polluted, broken, hurting city - just like there was hope for us. When we moved here in 2003, the drive into town was much different. I remember seeing tiny green trees sprouting up on the landscape, the rocks had been cleaned somehow, and the lakes in the area were open to residents for enjoyment.

I am a nature-lover and my environment can greatly affect my moods. I really connect with my outdoor surroundings. As I watched Sudbury continue to heal these past few years, I have watched myself and my husband heal. We have grown stronger - in each other and in our faith. Josh is back to work in a full-time pastor position at our church, we live in a wonderful house with a huge yard and lots of nature to enjoy, we've made some great friends, and our boys are happy.

It's been a long road, and our journey will continue until we meet Caleb in heaven one day. I don't know how long we're in this city of healing, but it's a beautiful place and we'll enjoy it as long as we're here.

February 4, 2004

Hi littlest one:

I want to write about you more. I've had an idea to make up a little booklet about miscarriage/stillbirth to give to churches - free material to hand out - then we'll see where that leads. Start with what God puts in my heart first and see where He takes it. There's really not a lot of material out there about this issue, especially not Christian material that someone could just grab and bring to someone who needs it. I'd love to reach those who share in the loss when it first strikes, while they gather other resources around them. That takes time. So that's the idea I have. Maybe asking a couple of other women to share their stories for the booklet because their stories are different from mine - to reach a broader scope of women/men.

    We went to the cemetery two days ago and your stone was covered in snow and ice - we couldn't even read it, nor could we find it for the longest time. I will get a special wreath for you so we know where you are. It really reminded me and hit home that you are not there, just your tiny body. You are free.

February 7, 2004

I blurted out the idea of this booklet to Josh and he likes the idea. Lord, may You be honoured and may our little Caleb be honoured. All in Your will. We just heard of a couple in town who lost a baby in the same way as Caleb - it just made me want to reach out. And hearing of them just increased my desire to reach out through the booklet. Even now open the hearts of churches to receive the booklet, Lord. May my vision for the words be Your vision and please may the words be Yours alone. Help me focus and hear Your voice only. This is important, I feel it - please keep me on the straight and narrow. I leave it all in Your hands, Lord. In Jesus' name. Amen.

February 11, 2004

Yesterday I had a hard time - funny thing - I was doing my books for the business for income tax. Going through the year's receipts - thinking on this day I had no idea we would lose Caleb just a month later. Then after - **wow** - I didn't do anything with the business for a month, or **wow** - I had to start back too soon - shipping something out just a month after. I went back and forth between pity and amazement at how God kept me going. It was hard to go through the past year and remember all the loss and all the change. Remember how it all changed Josh and I and how we were these past months. OK, then not good, then really not good, then OK again. Hard that just one year ago life was so different and the road we now travel is one we never imagined. Hard to get out of bed this morning. Did not sit to chat with Josh last night or reach out to him as he needs. And I need too. Just went to bed and **slept**. I still see Caleb everywhere - will it always be this way? At least now I fight the pity and depression, focus my eyes on Josiah and remember what I do have. One child here with me (for a long time I hope) and one in Glory. Still so sad sometimes. Still so hard. Still hurts so much.

CHAPTER 11
PREGNANT AGAIN?

If the future seems overwhelming, remember that it comes one moment at a time.
❖ *Beth Mende Conny*

How did we decide to try for another baby? Josh and I hoped for another sibling for Josiah and wanted to try one more time before we considered other options like adoption.

Was I nervous and scared through my third pregnancy? **Yes** and **Yes**!! Fear held me back for a long time - we didn't try again for fifteen months. Josh was ready before I was; I wasn't sure I could handle the situation of being pregnant after experiencing a stillbirth. But then a funny thing happened - one day I had a vision of a grown-up Caleb. He was pointing a tsk-tsk finger at me, as if he was saying, "Don't blame me if you don't want to try again, don't put that on me, you don't know what God is doing. If you want more kids, you go ahead and try, don't let ME stop you." Then I pictured myself having to answer to him in heaven. Strange, but it worked! I realized I was using Caleb as an excuse to hold back and there was only one way to face the fear. I was ready to try again. However, we also decided this would be my last pregnancy, whatever happened, whatever the outcome, because it was so hard emotionally.

Our pregnancy with Elijah was uneventful for the most part - we didn't experience any major life changes, and there were many blessings along the way.

I prayed for a good, wise doctor so that I could trust her judgment about how to handle different aspects of the pregnancy. I was considered high-risk because of Caleb's stillbirth, and I was cared for very well during my third pregnancy. I had more than the usual number of ultrasounds and doctor visits, my doctor decided to perform a c-section at 37 weeks as an added precaution against repeating our experience with Caleb, and I had many stress tests conducted at the end of the pregnancy. Despite all the wonderful medical care and concern, I was very anxious throughout the pregnancy. I found it hard to enjoy those few months, though I tried my best. I felt like I had been waiting forever to hold another baby of my own, and I couldn't wait for the day my third child was born, and I could hold them in my arms, healthy and whole.

When Elijah was born there were complications. Some babies are born weeks earlier than full term, and they are healthy enough to go home the next day. Elijah was born at just over 37 weeks and his lungs weren't quite developed. He had a small hole in his lung which caused a pocket of air to form outside his lungs, pushing on his heart and organs. He had to have a chest tube inserted and he was in the NICU for a week. I couldn't hold him for five days, couldn't hardly touch him because of the tubes and the discomfort he was experiencing.

My whole body longed to hold my son - I'd been waiting so long, too long, to hold another son. Here he was and I still couldn't hold him. So I prayed, knowing that the lesson in trusting God was not over, would never be over, and I waited for the outcome. I stayed in the hospital for four days as I recovered from the c-section, and I visited Elijah whenever I could. I saw him improve, little by little, and I started to let myself believe I would actually be bringing my little boy home soon. What a glorious day when I put him in his car seat, got in the car with my husband and drove Elijah to his new home. His first full day at home with us was the anniversary of Caleb's funeral two years earlier. Talk about God's perfect timing. I'm still amazed as I write about it.

SUBSEQUENT PREGNANCY CORRESPONDENCE

❖ EMAILS FROM THE HEART ❖

Following are excerpts from a correspondence between myself and a good friend who also experienced a stillbirth. (Find her story, *Catherine,* in the *Fellow Travellers on the Journey* section of this book.) The deaths of our second babies happened within a few months of each other and our subsequent pregnancies also happened within a few months of each other, so we were journeying through very similar stages at very similar times. These emails portray so well what was on our hearts during our third pregnancies...

May 13, 2004

Anna writing to Mary-Catherine around the 1st anniversary of Caleb's death:

Hi Mary-Catherine:

Thank you so much for your email - I have also been thinking about you, and wondering how you are doing... yes, the beginning of this month was quite challenging, and my mood dropped significantly, but has since improved. I have told people of my struggles, and asked for prayer, and I know God is hearing them!

Yes, we believe Caleb died on the 18th, I found out on the 19th, he was born on the 21st, and his funeral was on the 23rd - so I still wonder how I'll be next week - dreading it somewhat, but trying hard to focus on positive, on God.

I was recently "chatting" on msn with a friend, and was able to form these words to write: "I am trying to be submissive to Caleb's death, and God's will, even if I do not agree with it. I do not have to agree with it, but I do have to accept it." So that seems to sum up the past year - in many ways - Josh losing his job, Caleb's death, our move to Sudbury, the change in career for Josh - this has all been a challenge in submissiveness!

We are hoping to travel to see family in a couple of weeks and also visit the cemetery. Caleb's stone looks wonderful - we inscribed 'Surrounded by Glory' on it - also significant because the song that helps me so much, and we also played it at his funeral is I Can Only Imagine by Mercy Me – I'm sure you've heard it?! In this song it speaks of being surrounded by glory once we arrive in heaven. So Mary-Catherine, I continue to look beyond this world, anticipate meeting my son in my eternal home, and love him with all my heart though I cannot be with him.

Josh & I are getting closer to being open to trying for another pregnancy (Josh more so than me - pregnancy is not my favourite condition & I want to be more prepared mentally and physically to enjoy the process - no matter the outcome!) So we are planning for another go at it in the fall – I'd love your prayers on this one!

One way this month has already been redeemed (as you were hoping for me) - my sister just discovered she is pregnant with her first child! I am an auntie! And so life goes on, this year is another year, filled with new possibilities, and new futures.

Josh continues to seek God's will for employment. Josiah is growing more and more each day, and continues to be my greatest helper in healing and looking to what is ahead!

We just bought a house in Sudbury, a beautiful place with a big yard. So God's will is unveiling for us here in Sudbury & praise Him for all of it!

I hope your heart is good, Mary-Catherine, and you find yourself in a much better place emotionally, spiritually, physically, and mentally as each day goes by!

Much, much love to you dear lady!

Anna

May, 2004

Dear Anna:

Thank you for your e-mail. This past year has been such a whirlwind, I imagine, for you and your family. And like you, I do not necessarily agree with God's will for me (or for my little one), and I know that God is bigger, smarter and really more with it than me.

In reading your email, I too, recognize within me the challenge of "submitting" to God's will. In essence I have lately come back to remembering that I am creature, not Creator. And that means that I don't make the rules. I don't have the responsibility God has in the whole creation thing. My job is to love as I can, as best as I can. In spite of, and within, what happens.

We have struggled with having another child (or not). And what we kept coming back to was our individual and collective desire that our son have a sibling when we leave this planet. I'm 13 weeks along right now in another pregnancy. The experience has been humbling and challenging and healing and uncertain, with my emotions vacillating between hope and dread. Ah. I suspect that is normal for we who have experienced the loss of our little ones... I know that this will be my last pregnancy, regardless of what God wants to do with the little one within. So I wake up every day and welcome the little one, pray for health and a long life, and give the little one over to God. And being pregnant reminds me of my time with Catherine, how short it was, how it was difficult to enjoy her while I felt pervasively ill, and how I long to meet her (and will one day).

Anyway, my thoughts are with you this coming week especially. God has great plans for you and your family, Anna. The Creator of the universe has big plans for you! Good ones! May you experience comfort beyond imagining, peace that settles deep into your bones, and a sense of hope for the future that grows brighter each day.

With love, Mary-Catherine

June, 2004

Dear Mary-Catherine:

What a blessing you continue to be in my life... praise God for introducing us! I have read your email a few times these past weeks, drawing strength from your support, and from your understanding of my emotions. I must admit, I have not reached out to any support groups or anything of the sort, and when I try to explain my emotions to others who have never experienced the loss of a babe (thank God), it is hard to relate. So thank you for reaching out to me this past month.

I have been lifting you up in prayer for the pregnancy you are going through, for the little one that grows within you. Thank God for your words - for sharing how important it is to you that your son has a sibling, if it be God's will. When I read these words, they pierced my heart - Josh and I long for this also. And though I am so scared, it's almost time for us to try again - another few weeks. I have a feeling Caleb would not be too happy with the knowledge his mother and father were just too afraid to try again. I know he would not be pleased!

And now there's news from my sister that she is also pregnant - about 8 weeks now – already growing a belly. And I draw more strength from her - my little sis - and the new life growing inside her womb. So even though May started out pretty crappy for me - just reliving so many memories, dates, etc. the month was redeemed with the news of your baby and my sister's baby. I realized life goes on... the cycle continues... and I want to get back in the game.

I have mourned Caleb for a year, and will continue to do so for the rest of my life. But now, in order to honour him, I must keep going. I feel a huge weight lifted in getting past the one-year milestone, and now I have new memories of May, and they are good ones. So pray for us if you will, as we look towards trying for another baby. As I will pray for you, Mary-Catherine.

Thank you for sharing your news, know that I will be thinking of you and praying for you, and praise God for the blessing of the little one growing inside you, for your baby is proof that life continues, though we never know how God will use that life for His purposes. Thank you for encouraging me in your willingness to put yourself, once again, at God's feet and accept whatever He brings, and enjoy each moment that He gives.

Much love to you,

Anna

June, 2004

Dear Anna:

Thank you for your kind message. It is comforting to be upheld in prayer, and I thank you. And thank you, too, for sharing how May was for you. I have yet to come up to Catherine's anniversary date, and it is encouraging to read that it is possible to get through the rough stuff and feel a weight unburdening.

 I read in your email how you are seeking out life, and wanting to live life to the fullest. God has great plans for you and your family... and as I know in my own life, God's plans seem unfathomable and perplexing sometimes. And they are consistently better than my own. I will keep you and Josh in prayer as you navigate the waters of wanting another child, and opening that possibility to God.

 I'm at 17 weeks, and am working to live this day by day, and will be so relieved when the baby is born healthy and well. Ahhhh.

 My blessings go with you. And God has abundant grace and wonderful surprises just waiting for you.

My love, and hopes for good things for you, and my blessings,

Mary-Catherine

August, 2004

Dear Anna:

I am now in my 24th week and am feeling so much better than either of my other pregnancies... This pregnancy has been a rougher one than I anticipated... and has given me opportunity to come before God with my doubts and fears and uncertainties and questions. A good place to go, to be sure. And to rework my limited understanding of God... mostly it is a day to day thing, sometimes a week to week thing, and truthfully, sometimes hour to hour. And I focus on getting through this day/week/trimester, and letting God take care of the details and the outcome. When I remember who I am (creature, not Creator), it is much easier. Easier to let go, and let God.

October, 2004

How are you doing, Mary-Catherine? I am wondering how the pregnancy is going - hoping and praying all is well. I know you are coming up to your due date soon...I am about 6½ weeks pregnant myself... so I would love your prayers! My due date is June 4th - just one day later than Caleb's due date... I am hoping that God is working great and joyful things for these next few months - and that next May will be full of rejoicing, and not more sorrow.

I wait, surprisingly peacefully, and lay my heart and soul before my Lord, and see what He has for us... like you, I know He is good no matter what, and that He has plans for us and for the little one inside me. I'll keep you posted!

We are doing well, Josiah turned 3 in August, and we took him on his first canoe ride and his first overnight sleep in a tent - it was so much fun - we threw him a birthday party in the tent - complete with streamers, balloons, noisemakers, presents, etc.! What a constant joy he is to me - he keeps asking me how my baby is doing, and is it big yet? Then he pretends to take it out and hug and kiss it - already I can see how different this pregnancy will be for him, and how much more aware he will be of the changes in me. I am excited for him too.

October, 2004

Dear Anna:

My thoughts and prayers have been with you as you navigate this early pregnancy time. What a blessing for you and Josh. What a gift from God pregnancy is (although mine have felt more like trials by fire!). I'm currently 36 weeks + along and anticipating a c-section in 17 days. It has been a wild ride, this pregnancy, for lots of reasons, mostly because of Catherine's life and death. And the prayers and support of people around me have been such a blessing ... yours included, Anna. I hope to be a clear support to you in your journey, especially over the next number of months. Please keep me posted.

And I am so excited for you and Josh and Josiah. Congratulations! The God who watches over you and me, Anna, has good plans for us. And I hold in prayer before God the little miracle child you carry. May your pregnancy fly by at just the right speed, may your body feel strong, may the babe grow in health and beauty, may Josh and Josiah celebrate the process with you, and most of all, may God bless and keep you and the babe and your wee family.

My love to you across the provinces. It is a privilege to know of your new wee one, and to hold you in prayer.

Love,

Mary-Catherine

November, 2004

Dear Mary-Catherine:

I am 10 weeks along now - the baby is more than an inch long, and the nausea is already getting better - most days. I know there are many people praying for me, and I am thankful for that - there are many days when I feel I don't have the strength to do this again - just so much uncertainty - and then God asks me once again to leave it all with Him, and that He knows what's best, and that He loves me more than anyone else ever can. I know I am getting through each day of this pregnancy by God's strength alone - I am not relying on my own strength - it would not get me far!

November, 2004

Dearest Anna:

Thank you for your lovely message. My c-section is still... what, four days away, and I am on proverbial "pins and needles", anxious and worrying, and then remembering that God is bigger than me, has His arm around me (and always has) and has better plans for me than I know.

Reading your e-mail bumped me into the future when the wee one will be in my arms and I'll come to know more who she/he is. As I read your note about taking each day at a time in your pregnancy, my heart nodded in complete agreement. This is a time for you, as it has been for me, to remember who we are before God. Such a struggle that has been sometimes for me. Just as for me, I know that God has better plans for you than you do yourself.

And Caleb and Catherine, our wee heavenly babies, are having a blast, in the most loving arms beyond our wildest imaginations. I trust that these wee babes are fret-free, pain-free and love imbued. Kind of what I long for in my own life!

My prayers go with you in your pregnancy. It will be exciting to hear about your progress, and how you move along in this... both physically, emotionally and spiritually. You are a woman of strong heart, Anna, and I think that the experience of having to give a little one up too early to God is one that tries the strongest of souls. Whatever you need to do to maintain calm, mental health, joy, and to diminish worry and anxiety, I encourage you to do it. God knows your heart and what will strengthen you for the journey.

And wahoo! Ten weeks along is wonderful!

Summer 2005

Mary-Catherine writing to Anna - Elijah is now 2 months old.

How beautiful are your wee ones. I look at your littlest man's face and I wonder about the extra-radiant beauty that I see in him. Does God doubly bless us in the child who follows our "heaven's angel"? Our own little Elizabeth is such a precious soul, and I have wondered why God would have sent her to us... we certainly would not have met her if Catherine had lived (stopping at two seemed quite enough!).

August 27, 2005

I love you, little one, and I miss you always. I look forward to seeing you again and watching you play with your brothers. You have another brother now - Elijah Thunder. My 3 boys.

I am writing to say thank you. Thank you for all you have brought to my life - to our lives. Without you there would be no Elijah. I think we would have stopped at two children if you were here with us, but instead we have three gifts from God. And that's how I see Elijah - as a gift from you and from God. We visited the cemetery a few weeks ago and it was such a healing moment for me to take Elijah there - but your daddy still has a very hard time. I sat and I talked to you, like I always do, knowing that somehow God tells you what my heart says - somehow you hear me. We finally got your memory box all set up and put everything in it. From time to time I will look through and remember. But mostly I just carry you always in my heart and love you with all of me.

See you later angel boy,

Mommy

xoxox

CHAPTER 12

TEN YEARS ON THE JOURNEY

There is no grief which time does not lessen and soften.
   ❖ *Cicero*

I have a collection of blog posts and articles to share with you. They capture a few glimpses of the first ten years of our journey of healing…

June 2007

BALLOON LAUNCH 2007

In the May 2007 issue of the *Mom's Moments* newsletter, I wrote about our wee son, Caleb, who was stillborn in 2003. I shared our new family tradition, "On May 21st, we visit a playground, and take with us a helium balloon. We say a special prayer and we all grab hold of the balloon's string. Then we sing Happy Birthday, and we let the balloon go. We watch as it soars higher and higher, until we can't see it anymore, and we envision a balloon that reaches all the way to heaven, to our tiny Caleb, on his birthday."

Well… it's been a month since our balloon launch, and I think I'm ready to share a little about it. On May 21st of this year, we were driving back home from a visit with my family (Josh had gone away to B.C. for some leadership training, and I will travel great distances for some help with my two little men when their daddy's away!)

We stopped at a beautiful town, Parry Sound. We thought there was no chance of finding a helium balloon on Victoria Day - all the shops were closed. But God knows... and the dollar store in the mall was open, and had a wonderful selection of balloons, and a helium tank standing beside them, ready to make some memories for our family on this unique day. I said 'Thank you God', smiled, and asked my oldest son to pick whatever balloon he wanted for his brother. He picked a red one (his favourite colour), with four smiley faces on it ('How fitting!' I thought, because Caleb would have been four that day).

We walked out of the store, my son proceeded to let go of the balloon (not the launch we were hoping for!), we headed back into the store for another balloon, I held it tight, and away we went to the playground. We sat on the bleachers, sang Happy Birthday, kissed the balloon, and we all let go of it at the same time. We watched it soar, we thought of Caleb, we smiled a little and cried a little, then we played and played with the two boys God has given us to raise.

My heart grows every time I talk about Caleb, or write about him. I miss him so much, I know I always will, that feeling never lessens, and that's OK with me. It means that I'm his mommy and I love him. And I'm glad for our tradition, and red balloons with smiley faces...

❖ *Written as a blog post*

May 23, 2009

SIX YEARS AGO...

The day I write this, May 23rd of 2009, is the 6-year anniversary of the funeral of my middle son, Caleb. He was stillborn on May 21, 2003 and we held a wonderful memorial service for him on May 23 before we laid him to rest in the same cemetery plot as his great-grandpa Sklar.

Every year on May 21 we buy a helium balloon, find a scenic spot at a park or lake, sing Happy Birthday, and all four of us kiss the balloon before releasing it to the heavens. It's become a game to see who can keep the balloon in sight the longest. This year my littlest son yelled out "I love you Caleb!" as the balloon soared out of sight, and I almost cried. Almost. Not this year.

This year I'm tired of being sad. This year was really rough as I wrote out a small book in honour of my tiniest son. I'm so glad the project is finished for the most part, but I'm all out of tears. I want to look at Caleb's forever-too-short life with hope and excitement instead of grief and sorrow. I want to look forward to all the things he will do in the lives of others, all the people he will reach out to, all the hearts he will help to heal. I hope his story and our book will touch **tons** of hearts.

And that **excites** me! I want to stand back and watch how God will use Caleb to accomplish His purposes. I want to see with my eyes how good can come from bad. I want to be there when Caleb shines the light of God's love in the darkest places of grief and confusion.

Six years ago something **joyous** happened, something to celebrate. I had a beautiful baby boy named Caleb Joshua Freedom Sklar. May I never forget how blessed I am to be his mother. May I always hold my love for him in a special place in my heart. May I never stop discovering God's purposes for my son. And may I always remember I will meet him, know him, and love him even more when I reach my heavenly home. That gives me reason to jump for joy instead of weep with grief.

Pray for me if you will, that God will show me the next step for the book, that His purposes alone will unfold, and that my Caleb will bless others who are hurting.

I love you angel boy…

❖ *Written as a blog post*

October 9, 2009

THE WREATH

Every year I get a notice in the mail to order a wreath. This wreath is a very special wreath. It is for my middle son Caleb who was stillborn 6½ years ago. This wreath will sit atop his tiny gravestone and let us know where to find his resting place when the snow comes for the winter months.

I hate the annual letter that reminds me to purchase the wreath for another season. I hate that I have to make such a purchase, year after year, hate that it's a part of my life. I hate it because during the winter months I want to buy Caleb toys and books for Christmas and fill his stocking and see his face light up as he opens his gifts. Instead I'm buying a wreath that no boy would love to get on Christmas morning.

But I also love the wreath. I love that I have a tangible way to remember him every year. I love that when we visit the cemetery there is something there to signify that our Caleb is loved and remembered and cherished. I love to bring home a flower from the wreath and place it in a special spot in my house where I'll see it every day and smile. Why do I smile? Because I am full of hope.

I have hope that this Christmas, and every Christmas, Caleb will have no need to open gifts. His heavenly life is full of unimaginable beauty. And he enjoys the presence of the greatest gift ever given to this world – Jesus Christ. He doesn't struggle to remember Him in the midst of shopping trips, parties and recitals (all good things mind you!). He basks in His light and glory every second. And that's just cool.

So I'll purchase my wreath – in red this year I think, and I'll continue my love/hate relationship with the wreath, and I'll wish life was different, and I'll thank God for His provision for my heavenly boy, and I'll remember and cherish and love to the best of my ability. Always.

❖ *Written as a blog post*

November 3, 2009

FINDING HOPE AT THE CEMETARY

On Sunday we decided to stop in at the cemetery where Caleb rests in peace – it's very close to the Toronto Airport, and my husband was flying back in from classes at Wheaton College in Chicago. So the time seemed right.

If it was possible, I'd visit the cemetery much more often, but living 5 hours away provides a bit of a hindrance to those plans. It is still very hard for my husband to go there. The boys seem to be indifferent – they usually have a knack for making fun in any situation, if only we let them. Our 8-year-old understands why these visits are a part of our lives, and he doesn't complain about it. Our 4-year-old is just starting to try and wrap his brain around the notion of having another brother who lives in heaven. We have some **very** interesting talks about Caleb.

I was very happy to see the wreath already standing in its home for the winter. It looked so new, not weathered yet at all, tall and proud of the life it was remembering. I took my red flower and will add it to one of my plant pots at home. A little visual reminder of my tiny boy.

I'm hoping to make the cemetery visits mean something, instead of just sadness. So I suggested to Josh that we pray whenever we go. Pray for God's will and not ours for Caleb, and an understanding of what God will use Caleb's tiny life to accomplish in this world.

We sang a Sesame Street song and watched our boys play in the pine tree. They have their own ritual of collecting pine cones and decorating Caleb's stone with them. There were even some pinecones still in place from our last visit.

Maybe each visit will get a little easier, not because we miss him any less, but because we are starting to see hope.

❖ *Written as a blog post*

May 24, 2010

REMEMBERING CALEB

When May 19 – 23 rolls around every year, it is never an easy time for Josh and I. These few days mark the time between the discovery of the stillbirth of our middle son, Caleb, and laying him to rest in the cemetery.

May 19 is the day when the doctors couldn't find his heartbeat, May 21 is the day he was delivered, and May 23 was his funeral and burial. This year it began on a Wednesday.

Wednesday brought a bittersweet time as I helped a friend pack up her baby clothes to get ready for an upcoming move. I found a few precious items in the piles that I had passed along to her – clothes my boys have worn over the years, and the memories of them as I held those clothes again reminded me that God has given me two sons to raise, and one was His to raise. Caleb will never wear that Christmas outfit I remember buying 8 years ago for his older brother; instead he'll be forever clothed with the beauty of heaven.

Friday was Caleb's birthday and we launch a helium balloon into the sky every year. We go to a park with our sons, we pray, we all hold the string and kiss the balloon, we sing Happy Birthday and we let it go together. We see who can keep it in sight the longest – Josh always wins.

This year wasn't as sad as other years. This year Josiah had the idea to include jelly beans for Caleb, and Elijah wanted to include a verse. He picked one that we had read that morning. So we attached the candy and verse to the balloon string and we marveled at how our boys are making this celebration their own. Elijah shouted out "Here comes your present Caleb! Don't forget to get your present!" And I laugh and take joy in what I have, because that's the best thing I can do to honour my Caleb, and I blow a kiss to the heavens, and I watch my boys play at the park.

Sunday is the last day of the intense remembering. The day of Caleb's funeral and burial. This year we were at church and *Teen Challenge* was visiting. A wonderful ministry that helps men overcome their addictions and sets them free to experience God's love and new life. They share their stories and they sing. I love it when they visit.

As the service comes to an end, Josh spontaneously asks the men to sing one more song. They are caught by surprise but they pick a song – or should I say God picks a song and whispers it to them and they begin to sing... *I Can Only Imagine*. This was the song that spoke to our hearts the most during May 19 – 23 of 2003. This was the song that we played at Caleb's funeral. This was the song that inspired the words on Caleb's gravestone – *Surrounded By Glory*.

And as they sing God's gift to us that morning, I look at the men singing and I picture them standing beside Caleb one day and I see the look in their eyes when they realize how God used them the morning of May 23, 2010 at All Nations Church.

I am reminded of how much God loves us, and how seamlessly He weaves everything together. We just have to trust. We have to trust because there is nothing else to do.

And so our intense time of remembering Caleb comes to an end for 2010. It's been 7 years. It doesn't get easier, and I guess I hope it never does. But it does get better, fuller, more of joy than sadness, more of looking forward to meeting him than constantly missing him.

We will always remember Caleb, he is part of our family, he is part of our days, he is part of our hope, and he is part of our future. And that's always a wonderful thing to remember.

Love you angel boy – big kisses from Mommy!

❖ *Written as a blog post*

May 24, 2011

BALLOON LAUNCH 2011

May 21st is a special birthday in our house. It is the birthday of our middle son, Caleb Joshua Freedom Sklar, who was stillborn on this day 8 years ago.

We miss him immensely. That never goes away, nor do we want it to go away. It's just a part of loving a son who lives in heaven. A unique love is required, and we freely give it to our Caleb.

Balloon launches have always been our way of celebrating Caleb's birthday – we've done a launch ever since his first birthday. Most of them are done in Sudbury, and a couple of them were done out of town because his birthday usually falls on the Victoria Day long weekend. Other family members celebrate our Caleb with their own balloon launches in the places where they live. It's a special reminder of our special son, and balloons make it a child-friendly celebration so we can involve the young ones in our family.

We tell our boys (and my sister tells her children) about Caleb who is part of our family, but lives in heaven instead of with us. We tell them about hope – that Caleb lives with God and Jesus and the angels and lots of other people that love him. We tell them that one day we will meet him and it will be so much fun to play with him and talk to him.

It eases the sadness for us as we talk to the children about Caleb. Children always bring such hope. Our Caleb brings hope too. Hope for a world beyond this one. Hope for the future.

I wouldn't trade this intense missing him, these times tinged with sadness. There will always be this feeling along the fringe as we remember him.

We want it to be all smiles and laughter, but how can it be really?

At least it **is** possible to laugh and cry all at the same time – amazing how God made us so we can do that. We're such a jumble of emotion in our humanness, aren't we?

I know He laughs and cries with us, and that makes it all the more bearable.

Sometimes I feel like I don't know where to put Caleb in my heart. He doesn't fit with the other two boys who I get to see every day. I have to love Caleb so differently. I have to make a special place for him in my heart. The trick is not to leave him in there, separated from all the rest. I'm still fitting him in with the rest. Still. But I never want to stop letting him into everything, never shutting him away, letting my love for him touch **all** the rest.

Now, on to the details of Balloon Launch 2011.

This year Elijah sat down to write a note to his brother. Later we would insert it into the helium balloon before they blew it up at the store.

The note says: *I hope you have fun with God and Jesus.*

Amazing, isn't it? Straight from the heart of a little boy, and so real, and such a wonderful thought – that Caleb is having fun with God and Jesus on his birthday.

Josiah chose to include some jelly beans. After trying four jelly beans in the balloon, we realized only one could be inserted without weighing down the balloon. We needed it to float away for the launch.

We chose to release our balloon at the playground at the boys' school. They are closing the school next month, so we won't have another chance to release it from there in the future. And this is most likely where Caleb would have gone to school.

We all stood on the playground, sang Happy Birthday to Caleb, kissed the balloon and **let it go**!

It wasn't a very windy day, and the sky was clear, so the balloon took its time floating up to the heavens, and we were able to see it for a long time.

Hope you are having fun with God and Jesus today, Caleb.

Happy 8th Birthday.

Loving you, as always angel boy,

Mommy

❖ *Written as a blog post*

July 22, 2011

JOY COMES IN THE MORNING

No one ever wants to experience a night of the soul. None of us want to have days when we feel like our souls will never again see the morning light. Why would we ever seek to get stuck in the sadness, anger, loneliness or regrets of life? When we get stuck it feels like there is no way out.

There is a promise for you, for me, for all of us as we live through our nights of the soul.

For His anger lasts only a moment, but His favor lasts a lifetime; weeping may remain for a night, but rejoicing comes in the morning. - Psalm 30:5

My darkest night of the soul happened just after our middle son, Caleb, was stillborn. Eight days away from his due date, the nursery all ready, the bag all packed – then gone.

Night fell hard on me and it was pitch black. In the darkness I lost sight of myself, my life and my God. I wept in this new night. I wept a lot. I closed my eyes to the morning for a long while.

Yet even in the night, He held me tight. His arms enveloped me with a love that can stand any kind of darkness, even darkness that comes from dying on a cross. He whispered to me in the night, He told me He knew what it was to lose a child, He told me that the morning would come. He made this world so morning will always come. Morning even came after the tomb.

There was a full year of night. At first my dreams were dark, void of hope, full of loss. There were many who reached out to me in the night and shared similar stories. Their stories touched the blackness of my story and brought tiny rays of light. And over time, the dreams changed. They began to hint at something familiar.

Something that was still out of reach, but coming closer and closer. Something that looked like morning.

Slowly the darkness lifted. Slowly I lifted my eyes to the morning. I began to glimpse the pinks and oranges of His sunrise. His arms came out from around me but He never left me. Instead He held out His hand to me and we walked through those first rays of light. After a while we ran, skipped, jumped, and even laughed in the light. We danced joy's song in the full light of day. The music wasn't always happy and the dance was often slow and painful, yet it played on. Angels sang the melody. The hammering of nails to a cross kept the beat. The tune was eternal.

'His favor lasts a lifetime' means that even when my night fell hard and the dark was pitch black, joy was still with me. He is my joy and He is my morning. I may have lost sight of Him when there seemed to be no light, but He was still there. Joy held me tight even as I turned from Him. Joy shone His light even as I closed my eyes to Him. His favor scattered the long dark night and replaced my weeping with the joy of His people, His cross, His heaven and His hope. A song of hope that is ours for the dancing.

Night does return sometimes. Just as morning follows night, so night follows morning. I see the darkness returning every year on Caleb's birthday. Night sometimes comes when I see three brothers playing together, or watch the tears of baby-loss fall on another woman's face, or feel the soul-struggle of my husband at the cemetery. The weeping becomes part of us, but He helps us carry the hope and joy of His morning into the darkness of each night.

It will get better.

He knows no other way.

I just love His favor.

What helped me most in my darkest night of the soul:
- Surrounding myself with His people
- Immersing myself in His word
- Pouring out His music into my life
- Sharing the load, even when it hurt
- Doing anything I found uplifting
- Staying as healthy as I could

❖ *This is an article that was published in a magazine for Baptist Women*

May 22, 2012

BALLOON LAUNCH 2012
HAPPY BIRTHDAY CALEB!

Our Caleb would be nine on May 21, 2012.

It is a special task to celebrate the ever-too-short life of a child who has passed away long before his parents or brothers. Long before his grandparents, aunts, uncles and cousins. Long before his great-grandparents.

It's just not natural. It's just not right.

It's broken – like the world we live in. Fallen.

There are so many things that aren't right in this world. Yet God has promised to walk with us through every storm, every tragedy, and every hardship.

I have told you these things, so that in me you may have peace. In this world you will have trouble. But take heart! I have overcome the world. - John 16:33

And surely I am with you always, to the very end of the age. – Matthew 28:20

I have lived in the faithfulness and love of this promise for nine years.

So we celebrate – what else can we do with all the love in our hearts for our Caleb?

I am grateful for the short time we had. I am thankful that his soul touched ours, even for such a short time. I am confident of where he lives now – at home in heaven.

We talk about Caleb often in our family – he is one of us, and we openly talk about him – honest conversations. We talk about heaven, about boys that can't wait to wrestle their brother (I tell them to get ready because he may have had a few tips from Samson!), about a mommy that longs to feel her son's arms around her – picking her up and swinging her around in the biggest hug she's ever known, about a daddy who will one day look his middle son in the eyes and know that it's finally OK.

I chose a green balloon this year, and we went to Minnow Lake near our home. It was a very windy day and we knew the balloon would just shoot out of sight. I couldn't get a picture fast enough!

We all grab hold of the string and kiss the balloon. We sing Happy Birthday to Caleb. We release our gift to him – celebrating this day with him the only way we know how. We always see who can keep the balloon in sight for the longest time – Josh always wins.

We stand for a few minutes – each of us processing in our ways.

We do our best to love each other.

Somehow Caleb knows how much we love him.

This year Elijah wanted to use his Dairy Queen gift card to get a special treat for his brother's birthday. He also wanted to send a sundae up with the balloon, but I had to break it to him that the balloon wouldn't rise with a sundae attached. But it was a great idea! He also wanted to order an extra sundae and let it sit at the table with us. Another great idea, but sometimes I am very practical and didn't want to waste the food. Maybe next year we can order a sundae and give it away to someone in line?

And last night I opened Caleb's memory box with the boys. The one that Josh and his grandpa made, that a friend of ours painted with extreme care and love. It's beautiful.

We sifted through trinkets and treasures, through cards and poems. We talked more about him. We talked about good memories I have of that time – of people gathering around us and walking through with us – the hands and feet of Jesus to us – God with us, just like He promises. Then we read a book about heaven and it was time for bed.

I see how Caleb is changing our lives, our family, our world for the better – with the hope of heaven and the reminder of God's love and faithfulness.

I am proud of my son, honoured to be his mother, thankful, grateful for him.

The saying *It is better to have loved and lost than never to have loved at all* comes to mind.

I think it is true, but so hard to live through.

I would much rather love and keep.

So I love the two boys I have to raise, love them with all I am, with enough love for three boys all packed into two.

And I keep going, always closer to the day I'll meet our Caleb, knowing he would want me to live life to its FULLEST.

Somehow I know him, I know he loves me, I know he's waiting for me.

Smile. That is good for my mother's heart.

Happy Birthday to my heavenly boy,

Mommy

❖ *Written as a blog post*

May 22, 2013

BALLOON LAUNCH 2013

I'm still waiting for the happy ending. I'll be waiting for the rest of my life.

Yesterday was the 10th anniversary of Caleb's birth – his quiet, still birth.

Just as there was no hurrah or excitement or anticipation 10 years ago, there was none of that yesterday either.

There were 10 helium balloons, two confused parents with the same old questions, and two boys who are alive and well and happy. Thank God for them.

I guess I thought it would get easier by now, that there would be a few more answers or a lot more peace.

I guess I thought that 10 years would somehow be different, and feel different.

It's still the hardest thing in my life, I still don't have the answers, and peace still eludes me.

I have peace about where Caleb is, and I know that one day I will meet him. That fills me with indescribable joy.

I know that his story has helped and blessed and comforted more lives than I can count. That fills me with abundant hope.

It's quite simple, really.

I... just... want... him... here... with... me.

And that will never change.

❖ *Written as a blog post*

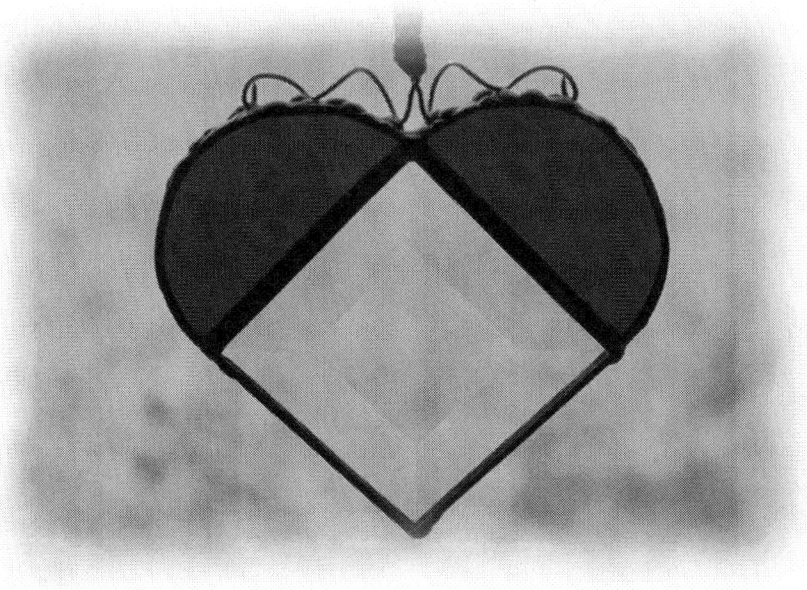

Part 3
Your Journey of Healing

HELP ME!

❧ CHAPTER 14 ❧

YOUR SUPPORT NETWORK

What an argument in favor of social connections is the observation that by communicating our grief we have less, and by communicating our pleasure we have more.
  ❖ *Sir Faulke Greville*

This is an article written by Kelly Gerken, the founder of Sufficient Grace Ministries for Women, Inc. She reaches out to offer comfort and hope to grieving mothers and families.

"Kelly and her husband, Tim, are the parents of five children: two boys who walk this earth with them and twin daughters and a son who are perfecting their dance in heaven."

It is often very difficult to know how to minister to the needs of a grieving mother who has lost her child. There are no magic words to take away the pain of such a loss, and many find it overwhelming just to look into the face of such suffering. Here are a few suggestions from a mother who has walked this path more than once.

- *Don't allow the fear of saying or doing the wrong thing keep you from reaching out in love. There are no perfect words. A simple "I'm sorry" and a hug can go a long way.*
- *Acknowledge the baby. Refer to the child by name. It is often a blessing to a grieving heart to hear her child's name spoken. Do not think that talking about him/her will bring the mother more pain. The memory of her baby is always on*

her mind. Sharing can be a comfort. Be willing to listen. She may need to tell her story over and over again.

- Those who are grieving are not always able to ask for help. Instead of saying, "Let me know if you need anything," just do something for the mother and her family. Be available, but also be willing to give space when needed. Bring a meal. Offer to watch the other children for awhile. Come over and sit with her, offering a listening ear.

- Realize that your friend has been forever changed by the loss of her baby. Don't expect her to be exactly the same. And please realize that grief has its own time table. Allow her the time she needs, and remain supportive. Everyone grieves differently. Don't judge her choices or her "performance". She may not react the same way that you think you would.

- Avoid clichés such as "You can have more children" or "This was God's will". Even words meant to comfort can actually sting a grieving heart like salt poured into an open wound.

❖ Kelly Gerken, Deshler, Ohio

Blog: **http://blog.sufficientgraceministries.org**

Website: **www.sufficientgraceministries.org**

CHAPTER 14
FELLOW TRAVELLERS ON THE JOURNEY

For this part of the journey, we're just going to sit and rest a while. We're going to share our stories and shed our tears and discover our hope – together.

This is Mary-Catherine's story – you may remember walking and talking with her for a while in the *Pregnant Again?* section of the book. She shared her story with Anna through email in December 2003…

CATHERINE

I gave birth to our stillborn daughter Catherine on October 3, 2003.

I was due to have a c-section just 11 days later.

The similarity of your experience around Caleb was both surprising and comforting.

Catherine had been in a "frank breech" position for a couple of weeks, and an ultrasound at 35 weeks showed that she was healthy and quite stuck... her ankles were up around her ears, with her legs stretched out. Consequently I couldn't feel her move (because she couldn't!) for two weeks.

When the oby/gyn (at the 37 week appointment) said he couldn't find the heartbeat I didn't know if he was actually looking at the right spot... as the nurse in the week before hadn't been able to find her heartbeat at first due to her breech position (and the placenta being at the front... whatever that means!). But he brought in a portable ultrasound machine and confirmed that she had both turned head down (sometime within the week) and no longer had a heartbeat. It has been a long haul since that moment.

The last few weeks have been dark times indeed, and only recently have I seen a light (intermittently) through this (long) tunnel of mourning.

Having grieved for the death of both my father (when I was 21) and my mother (shortly before we met), the path of grieving seems all too familiar. And I know that it is only by faith that I will come through this a better, stronger and more alive person. Trusting that God has purpose beyond my own is something I cling to, and as yet do not understand (and likely will not understand until I meet God face to face).

I know that God's grace is with me now, even when I can't feel it, understand it, or even appreciate it... the commonality of the experience of losing a little one before/during/shortly after birth is a unique one... and that connecting with other women/families who have experienced the same can be (and has been for me) a blessing.

In the meanwhile, the process of grieving continues... and I sense week by week that I am coming to new places. Jesus has been kind to me in the journey of grief. I hope that you experience the same kindness and mercy, Anna.

❖ *Mary-Catherine*

LORD, WHY ME?

I remember the day our doctor confirmed that we would be expecting our first child. My husband Gerry and I were living in Ottawa, Ontario.

At our first ultrasound the nurse began to observe the baby. "Ah ha, there's the baby! See the head and arms? Listen to the heart beat." "Thump! Thump!" How exciting!

But in minutes, our hopes and dreams came crashing down. Something was wrong! They discovered a sac of fluid behind the baby's head. The doctor wasn't sure what it was but gave only two possible solutions: there would be a cure or the baby should be aborted. We were shocked at this news.

I was referred to the General Hospital where further testing revealed that our baby girl had Turners Syndrome. While devastated by the news, we were still hopeful because TS was not life threatening. However, as weeks went by and as more tests were done, they discovered that she also had a bad heart.

The doctors gave us two new options: the first required a series of three operations in the first year of her life; the second required a heart transplant. Again, we were devastated but still held out hope.

March 20th, 1991, Ashley Victoria Gould was born. Immediately, the doctors ran some tests and discovered that her heart was worse than they had anticipated. Nothing more could be done for Ashley. She died the next day.

"Why God? Why would You allow this? Why me?"

We wrestled with these questions. Through the painful experience of losing Ashley, this is what we learned: God loves us and will not put anything in our lives that we cannot handle. We live in a fallen world where tragedy is going to happen. If we look to Him, God draws close to us in our pain.

Suffering developed our character (compassion, patience, longsuffering). Today, we are more sensitive to those who are going through pain. We see some purpose through it all – that God is using our loss to touch the lives of others for eternity and to further His kingdom. It also has made us look forward to that day when the Bible says there will be no more pain, sorrow, tears and death.

Gerry and I came to a defining moment in our journey. We faced the choice either to become bitter or to completely depend on and trust God, allowing His will to be done in us. We chose the latter, and through it all, experienced God's presence and promise (see Psalm 29:11).

❖ *Leah Gould, Richmond Hill, ON*

Leah has 3 teenage children, and her husband Gerry is the lead pastor of Summit Community Church.

FINDING FAITH IN DIFFICULT TIMES

My husband, Daniel, and I both grew up in North York, Ontario. We were just teenagers when we started dating, and we married at age 21. Daniel believed in God (although not a practicing christian at the time) and I was a self-proclaimed atheist.

Daniel had a good job working with race horses on the family farm in Uxbridge, where we eventually moved.

Our family began when our first child Ryan was born; I felt privileged to be able to stay at home with him. The farm was a beautiful place to raise a child, we were surrounded by horses, and Daniel's work was just outside our front door. I recall Daniel walking a horse right up to our living room window for Ryan to see!

When Ryan was 2½ yrs old we had another baby. This time a beautiful little girl we named Jennifer Ashleigh. She had dark hair like Daniel, and she was born on her Grandpa's 50th birthday. It was 1989 and the song "Dream Come True" played over and over in my mind the day after she was born.

When Jennifer was just 6 weeks old she began to lose strength. We took her to the doctor who recommended a neurologist. After 3 weeks of testing they informed us that Daniel and I were both carriers of a matching defective gene for Spinal Muscular Atrophy (SMA), which we had passed on to Jennifer. They told us that Jennifer would only live for 6 months. I hyperventilated in the doctor's office when they said she had what was known as "floppy baby syndrome". Jennifer's muscles would continue to degenerate and she would lose the ability to suck, swallow and eventually breathe.

The disease did not affect Jennifer's brain, she smiled a lot, and was usually quite content and happy (you see - she didn't know that she was supposed to be able to move her limbs). We would keep her in the bath for as long as she liked each day, because it allowed her body to move freely.

Ryan couldn't fully comprehend what was happening (thank goodness), he adored his sister and would lift her hands in the air, and sing to her, "Hands up... baby hands up, gimme your heart..."

At 2 months of age Jennifer was too weak to breastfeed any longer and started bottle feeding, eventually she was fed by tube. I began experiencing major anxiety and panic attacks, Daniel started to drink a lot. My doctor explained that the anxiety was caused by the upset in the "natural order of life" – children usually outlive their parents!

Our family and friends surrounded us offering strength and support! We were blessed with 4 great sisters and 1 wonderful brother between us. Our parents did all they could to help. Daniel's Dad began to plan a children's charity in Jennifer's name so that her memory would live forever.

Jennifer died in October '89 at 6 months of age. At her funeral, I asked Daniel to make sure that Jennifer was buried with her blanket wrapped around her. All I could think of was that winter was coming, and it was cold outside. Daniel's christian family was sure that she was already in heaven. I needed desperately to find out if God and heaven were real.

The year following Jennifer's death I began a journey of attending church, reading the Bible, and I did a study on "Creation vs. Evolution". I started to pray, and God answered my prayers! My life changed so much in that time; without God, I don't know how I would ever have my joy restored, but it was, **fully**!

In 1991 we had another baby girl (Danica); sadly she too had SMA and passed away at 5 ½ months of age. Ryan has been a great blessing to us over the years; he is 20 years old now and healthy as a horse! I jokingly say… "yesterday I laid him in his crib and he was 6 lbs 13 oz… this morning, I woke up and he is 6 feet tall and nearly 200 lbs".

Daniel quit drinking for good 6 years ago, at which time we were both baptized in our new church, together.

Children are indeed a gift from God, they belong to Him and we may have them for a short time or a long time… only He knows.

❖ *Mary Clements*

For more information on the foundation created by Mary's family, *The Jennifer Ashleigh Children's Charity*, visit **www.jenash.org.**

THE LEAST OF THESE

The cardiologist walked into the room, glanced at my chart and asked, "So you didn't get an abortion?" As I was 34 weeks pregnant, it seemed an unnecessary question.

For one agonizing night we actually considered it. Twenty-two weeks into my second pregnancy we learned the boy I was carrying had Down Syndrome and a serious heart defect. Though my husband and I detested the idea of abortion, we wondered if we were cruel to let him live. On April 17, 1996 we sat in our living room, numb with shock. "What if sparing him suffering is the only thing we can do for him?" Keith asked our minister, Duke Vipperman, who had come by to talk to us.

"You sound as if you believe it is you who are causing his suffering," Duke replied. Then he explained that we do not cause suffering, it just happens. Those closest to God, who are most at peace, are often those who have suffered the most. "If you try to ease his suffering by denying him life," Duke told us, "you are in essence saying you can do God's job better than God."

For Keith this settled the issue. He had never wanted to abort, but as a physician he wanted to "fix the problem"-- to make sure he was doing all he could for our baby.

I knew I could never go through with an abortion, but it was not just because of my moral objections. I had felt him kick. Even though he was small, I sensed him fluttering at only 14 weeks, and he just kept growing more active. I could never abort him. I loved him. He was my son.

Christopher arrived eleven days early on August 6, 1996. Suddenly he was no longer a medical problem but a tiny bundle who breathed a little too fast, and who stared into my eyes with recognition and, I think, love.

His first two weeks were peaceful ones, as he was healthier than we expected, and we learned all the facets of his personality. He enjoyed being cradled and listening to singing, but would kick and scream in indignation if he lost his soother. When our 1½ year old daughter Rebecca visited him, she would lean over the bassinet, pat his blond fuzzy head and say, "My baby?" I would nod, and promise that we would take him home soon.

But we couldn't. As his heart began to fail Christopher grew increasingly tired and lost weight instead of gaining it. He was transferred to Toronto's Hospital for Sick Children to await surgery.

During the evening, as I sat alone with him in his room, I would hold him and whisper, "Do you know how much Mommy loves you?" Babies, so tiny and helpless, inspire a purer love than most. It is an unselfish love, since babies--and especially those who are sick--cannot promise anything in return. I am a goal oriented person, yet with Christopher, I learned to sit and just "be". I had no choice. And in the quiet, I sensed God whispering His own unconditional love to me, too. "Thank you, God," I whispered, "for the chance to know this precious boy."

Usually his room was bustling with visiting friends, relatives, and Keith's colleagues. We even held a dedication service there. The event was somber, for though we were celebrating his life, we all could see how tiny he was for the battle that lay ahead. The doctors gave Christopher a 25% chance of post-operative survival, for he was only 4½ pounds.

On the morning of his surgery I was terrified I wouldn't hold him again. "I want so much more for you, honey," I said. "But I am glad to have the chance to love you. No matter what happens, I will see you again."

For five days he recovered well, and the doctors grew optimistic about his chances. But on September 3

Christopher's breathing again grew rapid. That night my mother watched Rebecca, and Keith and I visited him together. "Mommy loves you, sweetheart", I whispered as we left his room. It was 9:30 p.m.

He was only 29 days old when he died later that night.

The number of people at the funeral amazed us. Along with family and friends, many from the hospital attended, too. We asked Duke to talk about the importance of Christopher's life, as we felt so many had discounted him because of his disabilities. "We must not look down on little children, for they are our model of God's kingdom," Duke preached. Jesus Himself chooses to identify with them, for whoever welcomes them, welcomes Him (Matthew 18:5). "Christopher was what we are to be: a little one, utterly dependent on God, struggling against apathy and everything that would deny us the sweetness of life."

The two years since his death have been full ones. I have shed many tears, but I also smile now when I remember him. We have a new baby girl, and Keith is establishing his own pediatric practice. I often think about how different life would be had I aborted him. I would have no memories and no peace. And how do you talk about your pain? People understand my pain when I say I had a baby who died.

I can visit him at his grave. But most of all, I can look my girls in the eyes and tell them with conviction that I love them unconditionally. And they believe me, for I loved him.

Many may think his was a wasted life. He never came home from the hospital, he never smiled, and he was rarely even awake. But they didn't watch the faces of his grandparents when they held him, the nurses as they watched us, or the people we have comforted since. They do not know how Christopher changed us. And so they cannot see that his life is much more than those 29 days. Recently Rebecca told me not to be sad, because Christopher is in heaven, and he is happy now. I think she is right. And one day we will meet him again, and the blessing that was his life will be complete.

❖ *Sheila Wray Gregoire is a writer and inspirational speaker. She is mother to four - two in heaven and two on earth.*
  http://www.sheilawraygregoire.com
  http://tolovehonorandvacuum.com
  http://facebook.com/sheila.gregoire.books

LIZZIE'S STORY

It's Mother's Day as I write this and while the world and my family will celebrate me for being the mommy of two beautiful girls, in my heart I will always be the mommy of three. My eldest daughter Elizabeth was born July 3, 2001 and died hours later on July 4, 2001.

My husband and I ventured into parenthood just as so many others do - happy and naive. We laughed at my morning sickness and were delighted by her strong kicks. Then, in the twenty-third week, tragedy struck unexpectedly.

It was the first long weekend of the summer and we were spending our first night of the season at our cottage. In the early morning hours of that first night there, I awoke suddenly, instinctively knowing that "something wasn't right". I called the hospital and was told to get some rest. I called back minutes later insisting that we were on our way to see a doctor. I waited in that rural hospital for an agonizing eight hours before I was sent by ambulance to the nearest hospital with more specialized care. By the time of my arrival there, eleven hours had passed since my initial call and labor was too far progressed. Delivery was imminent.

Five hours later, our Elizabeth Grace was born. She was tiny yet perfect, like a doll but with a strong heartbeat. We questioned why nothing was being done to help her breathe easier but the hospital wasn't equipped to deal with such tiny babies. We had no options other than to keep her comfortable and watch her fade away from us.

Many of those hours we spent with her remain a blur to me. I don't think I counted her fingers or toes and I'm not even sure I told her how much I loved her. I do, however, remember holding her, singing to her and watching her being baptized. I also remember the moment she died. I didn't tell anyone right away that she had passed on. I wasn't ready to give her up. My husband and mom were the first to notice that something was amiss. I confirmed their suspicions and whispered to them, "She's gone."

In the days following her death, we were busy making funeral arrangements and receiving calls from family and friends. Born so prematurely, nobody knew her but us and nobody really knew what to say. It was often uncomfortable on both ends but we were grateful for the consideration. I comforted myself by thinking that she was just too fragile to live in this (at times) harsh world. Nothing else seemed to make sense to me at the time. The well-meaning platitudes certainly didn't help; "It was meant to be", "It was God's will", "You'll have others". Why was it meant to be? Why would God choose my baby? Will I have others and is that even relevant?

Raised in an evangelical home, I didn't want to question God, but I was no longer certain that I wanted to believe in a God who "willed" babies to die. While making the arrangements with our pastor, he assured me that God was more than capable of handling my anger. He and our compassionate funeral director validated my feelings and allowed me to feel cheated and bitter.

Over time, my scattered thoughts have calmed and the raw edges of pain have softened. I don't think God 'willed' my baby to die. I think God in particular never intended babies or any of us to die. But we live in a fallen world, and time and chance can happen to us all. I believe God can help me decide how I'm going to cope with this profound loss and learn about life in the process. I once read a best-seller that likened one's life to a fine tapestry. Beautiful from the front, but a jumbled tangled mess of threads at the back. Perhaps one day I'll be able to look at the beautiful life I've experienced because of the trials I've endured.

About a year after Elizabeth's death, I became pregnant again. It was a difficult journey and paranoia was at every corner. At twenty-three weeks, I went into premature labor once again. What they thought was coincidental in my first pregnancy was now forming a pattern. Our doctors began preparing us for the worst-case scenario but this time we were not going down that path again without a fight. We were determined not to bury another baby.

While I was in the hospital in Trendelenburg position (head down-feet up), Jeff pored over research journals on the internet and found a special pregnancy program. Against medical advice, I was flown to Toronto where I underwent surgery and labor was halted.

I remained on bed rest there for an additional five weeks before I gave birth to a small but healthy baby girl. While other parents around us lamented about having a preemie in the NICU, we rejoiced. We knew Emma would face life-threatening challenges ahead of her and that her hospital stay would be lengthy, but she was alive! We spent every waking moment with her in the hospital for two months until the day came that we could finally take her home. What a blessing it was to take a baby home after all we had been through.

Since then, we've had our third daughter, Brianna. After many consultations, appointments, injections, ultrasounds and even a temporary relocation, she was born a healthy, full-term baby.

Because of Elizabeth, we knew I was at risk with Emma and became proactive in fighting for her life. Because of Emma and Brianna, we learned that I have a rare clotting disorder and require blood thinning medication. My blood especially clots during pregnancy which clogs up the placenta and triggers preterm labor. The combined information from all three pregnancies came together to solve the puzzle. Solving this puzzle has potentially saved my life and will almost certainly spare my girls the same heartbreak in their future pregnancies.

As time marches on, as it inevitably does, there isn't a day I don't think about how Elizabeth has touched my life. It's the capacity in which I do this thinking that has changed. In the early days, I'd sob at the thought of all the early memories. Memories of her tiny lifeless body in my arms or the heart wrenching memory of her small white casket being lowered into the earth. How do you say good-bye to your child when you've only just begun to say hello?

There are still painful days, but now when I think of her I often reflect upon how she's changed me as a person. I think I'm a better person for having her in my life. I'm kinder, more compassionate and above all else, humbled by the fragility of life. Every life, no matter how brief, has a purpose. Though her time on this earth was short, her legacy will live on in me and those that loved her. Perhaps she accomplished in a few hours what some of us do in a lifetime.

I believe I'm also a better parent because of her. I enjoy my children and try to cherish every crazy, chaotic moment with them. I've also learned the true value of a good friend. I lost a few friends as I grieved but I also gained a few gems. Women I never would have met except that we all belonged to the same unfortunate 'club'. A club that nobody cares to join - the club of lost babies. Together we've laughed, cried and found hope. Together we've found a safe place where we can remember our babies and speak their names. Today is one such baby's birthday. I think of him up there in heaven with Elizabeth and smile at the thought of the two of them orchestrating a 'meeting of their moms'. Though I never met him, he was fundamental in helping me heal. His mom patiently and tenderly guided me through the muddy waters of grief.

Finally, Elizabeth's life has taken away the sting of death for me. I no longer fear death or dying. I anticipate a great reunion with my daughter some day. What a joyous day that will be! For now, one thing is for certain, a piece of my heart will always belong to Elizabeth. She's one of "my girls"; the one who is always missing in family photos and whose name is rarely spoken.

So as this Mother's Day draws to a close, I think of all those "invisible mothers" with "invisible children" and whisper a silent prayer for them. I pray that they will make it through another painful day and that they too will find hope and faith in their lives once again.

❖ *Anonymous*

SIX BABIES

Having a miscarriage never crossed my mind... then it happened to me.

Four times.

I share the following journal entries with you in hope that my story might make a difference to someone.

August 24, 2011

Last night I tucked my three-year-old into bed but she wasn't ready to sleep. After a couple of, "Can I have a glass of water?" requests, and "Mommy, can you check on me?" questions she looked at me and said, "Mommy, I want to be a big sister".

I'm holding back tears as I write this. I told her that I thought she'd be a great big sister and that she could ask God to make her a big sister. Her eyes lit up so I went on to explain that God is good and we can trust Him -- if she asks He might say yes and that would be very good but He might say no and that would be very good too because God loves us and He is good. He will make the best choice for us. We can trust God. Then I tried explaining how God grows a baby in a mommy's tummy and I ballooned my shirt out to explain that if I had a baby I'd be big for a long time and we laughed. In the end I encouraged her to pray and said it is up to God. I think I handled it well.

'What's the big deal?' you might be wondering.

I have been pregnant five times but I only get to raise one daughter. 2007. 2010. 2010. 2011.

Aurora, my light, was born on August 13, 2008.

She has four siblings we'll never know this side of heaven. I don't want her to grow up alone. I don't want an only child. Apparently she doesn't want to be an only child.

It's not up to me. I'm trying. John and I are trying but we haven't gotten pregnant yet. And my menstrual cycle has changed. I'm worried. I'm aching. So sad.

My only hope is in God. I know He is good. I know He loves us. I will trust Him. We want another baby but we will accept being a family of three if that is God's plan for us.

The first time I got pregnant was in 2007. I couldn't imagine anything going wrong and so we shared our news. I started bleeding and cramping. John took me to the hospital. After being examined and a very long wait I had some terrible cramping and lost my first child. My baby was barely nine weeks old. We were very sad.

Ever the optimist I was ready to try again soon. We got pregnant quickly and I gave birth to Aurora in August 2008.

In 2009 we were ready to try again ~ completely confident that our next pregnancy would be just as healthy as when I carried Aurora. We shared our news and like every pregnancy I was violently ill. At the three month mark I started to lightly bleed.

On New Year's Eve 2009, at a friend's house, I squatted down at the coffee table and I felt like my water had burst. I was bleeding badly. I insisted on going home where John put Aurora to bed and I sat on the toilet talking on my cell phone to my midwife. Then I passed out. John caught me and I woke up in the bath tub with John watching me and talking to the 911 operator. I was carried out of my home in an embarrassing, half naked, bloody mess, put on a stretcher and taken to the hospital in an ambulance. I chatted and joked with the paramedics… I think this is my personal defense mechanism because it was a horrible experience.

Lots of exams, an overnight or two and one D&C later I was released from the hospital with no explanation and no baby. God bless Aurora, she slept through it and our friends came over with their daughter so John could come see me. My dear friends, only months before, had also miscarried.

I was told to wait and have a normal period or two before trying again. We were terrified but went for it anyways. We decided that "there is no fear in love" (1 John 4:18) and that we would not be afraid. As soon as possible we tried again.

In June of 2010, again at the three month mark, I started bleeding. At the hospital I had another D&C. Fear tore at us.

After losing a baby there is a lot of healing that needs to take place: physically, mentally, emotionally and spiritually. After a couple months I was mostly physically recovered. Mentally I always think practically and I also had to brave a good attitude for my wee girl. I chose to do a lot of reading, to set up doctor appointments, and to pray a lot. I took one day at a time.

In July of 2010 I felt terrible. I wrote this poem:

An ache I can't articulate
He knew you. I lost you.
I love you. He loves you.
He holds you. I miss you.
My children are in heaven
I am here on earth-
with one child instead of more.
with my husband.
with time and breath.
with hope.
with fear.
with love.
with an ache I can't articulate.

I asked myself "Why? Punishment? Is my body broken? God doesn't trust me with more? Am I not good enough? A bad mother? No. Will I be okay? My body? Can I... should I try again? Unfair. Undeserving. Still thankful. Still hopeful. Can my faith withstand anymore? At my breaking point."

John and I knew we needed more time to heal. When we finally felt ready, in early 2011, I got pregnant again. And again our baby died. Barely two months and I miscarried.

We have no answers. With every miscarriage I spend a lot of time stuck in bed. I pray, read, watch movies. Mostly I feel very sad and wish I could make a plan. Do I sell the baby stuff or keep it? Should I grieve for my babies? Can I have more? Is this a lesson in patience?

In 2010, Aurora kissed my pregnant belly and said, "Bye". Days later I miscarried. Coincidence? I don't know but God used the moment to start preparing my heart to say goodbye.

Each of these losses has required a grieving period. We are very open with our lives and emotions. Talking helps me to process my thoughts and feelings. John needed to talk too but he sought counseling. I don't think how you deal with losing your baby matters as much as the fact that you need to deal with your terrible new reality.

There are things I didn't expect:
- ❖ to cry in the baby department
- ❖ to be both extremely happy for and jealous of friends and their newborns. (especially those having second babies)
- ❖ talking to our extended family about their grief
- ❖ feeling so stressed about my health (is there something wrong with me?)

- responding to:

    "so did the doctors tell you what's wrong?"

    "maybe it's for the best"

    We're still trying. We'd like to have at least one more baby. Twins would be wonderful! God is giving me peace and reminding me by scripture and by people around me that God is good and that we can trust Him and His plans.

    God blessed us with Aurora. He has healed us. Now our struggle is the unknown. But we choose to trust Him who is faithful and who loves us.

March 23, 2012

I am six months pregnant! My first trimester was hell. I was so sick I couldn't get out of bed and had to take a leave from work. The doctor says we are having a girl. We've named her Keely.

I was terrified of losing her the whole time I was sick. Even when (maybe especially when) I started to feel better. Slowly 'hope' returned. God is crushing the fear in me. Aurora is getting the baby sister she asked for. This fills me with joy!

July 9, 2012

Keely is born. She is a beautiful gift.

- *Brittany-Ann Austin*

STACEY'S STORY

After 10 long months of trying, it finally happened. God had answered our prayers. I woke up very early in the morning and took the test. It was positive! I was so excited I barely knew what to do with myself.

I had thought of this moment since I was a little girl... and I wanted to make sure that it was memorable (as if finding out that you are carrying a tiny being inside of you can be any less memorable!).

So, I emptied the closet in our guest room where my husband hung his clothes, threw everything on the bed and hung up this tiny little newborn onesie with a sign that said "Make room Daddy, I'm moving in!"

After that, I climbed back into bed and impatiently waited for Johnson to wake up. I may have even rolled around and nudged him a little more than usual. After what seemed like an eternity of him going through his normal morning routine, he **finally** made his way to the closet.

I stood in the doorway holding my breath. He opened the door and just stood there, staring inside for the longest time. Then, he looked at me and said, "Really?!"

It was a rollercoaster of emotions – tears, laughter and everything in between that would start our journey towards parenthood.

Three weeks after that precious moment, I lost the baby. I was 7 weeks pregnant. The Doctors and staff were all very kind and did their best to assure me that there was nothing I did wrong or that I could have done differently. "Sometimes, things just happened this way," they said.

Although they meant well, their words brought me no comfort and nothing anyone said or did could fill the void that I felt so deeply. I tried to find comfort in knowing that God had a plan for me and if I trusted Him, things would work out.

Two months later, we found out we were expecting again. This time, the joy wasn't as overwhelming as it was the first time around. This time, there was also accompanying feelings of fear and worry.

Johnson wanted to keep the pregnancy from everyone this time around – until we were "sure" nothing could go wrong. My reaction was the complete opposite. I needed our close friends and family to know – so that they could be there to support me if something happened again. I didn't think I could handle feeling as alone as I did that first time around. We agreed that we would wait until the 8 week ultrasound before making the announcement. A good compromise.

When the time for the ultrasound came around, I was so nervous! When the technician said that she could see a heartbeat, I let out the most relieved sigh and couldn't help the tears from coming. We did it. We beat the dreaded 7 week mark. We excitedly called those closest to us to share the news. It was wonderful to finally be able to share our joy a little.

Two weeks after that, during a work trip to Thunder Bay, I started spotting. I was nervous and felt that something was wrong. I drove myself to the hospital and to my horror was told that there was no longer a heartbeat. I couldn't believe it. I honestly believe that at that very moment, God took over and allowed me to "keep it together" long enough to make my way home.

It wasn't until my husband met me at the airport with a beautiful bunch of flowers that I wasn't able to control myself any longer. I couldn't stop sobbing and apologizing for putting him through this again. I was heartbroken. The ordeal wasn't over for us either. I had to wait for everything to pass naturally.

Later that night, it finally happened…but I also started hemorrhaging. My husband had to call the ambulance and stand by helplessly while they took care of me. The hospital staff were amazing and were very sensitive to our situation. They were able to remove all the left over tissue and send me home to rest.

The emotional and physical ordeal was a lot for us to take. We had a long discussion over whether or not having children was for us. Johnson didn't know if he could go through all of that again but I knew that I was meant to be a mother and that it would happen for us someday.

Two short months after that awful night, God blessed us with a little miracle one more time. Although that pregnancy also had it's fair share of ups and downs, on August 19th, 2012 we were able to hold God's Grace in our arms.

Our beautiful healthy baby girl was and is everything we could have ever dreamed of and more. I'm not sure why those two awful miscarriages had to be part of our story, but whatever the reason, we feel even more blessed to have a beautiful daughter that brings so much joy to our lives everyday.

When I got pregnant after Grace, I have to admit that I thought my pregnancy drama was over. I was wrong. At only 5 weeks, I lost my 4th pregnancy.

I'm not sure if it was because this miscarriage didn't carry as much trauma as the last one did, or if it was because I had come to terms with the fact that I would someday meet those precious little ones that God decided to hold near to Him, or maybe it was because I could see all the wonders of the world in my daughter's eyes... but it was possible to surrender that little life to God and hope that I would someday carry another little baby in my arms. Not easy – but possible.

I am now 27 weeks pregnant with another baby girl and we can't wait to meet her. Every day I am thankful for the beautiful family that I have been blessed with. I think of my angel babies often and wish I could have had a chance to meet them, hold them, and tell them stories about their Heavenly Father. Every day, I take comfort in the fact that He has greeted them, He is holding them and He is teaching them about me.

❖ *Stacy Sathaseevan*

❦ CHAPTER 15 ❦

PRACTICAL IDEAS

THE HOSPITAL

Though I Walk through the shadows
And I, I am so afraid
Please stay, Please stay right beside me
With every single step I take
   ❖   *Need You Now*, Plumb

If a hospital visit is part of your journey, these ideas may be of some help during a difficult time...

- ❖ Share the news with a couple of close friends or family members, and then ask them to make the rest of the calls.

- ❖ Ask for a hospital room that is farthest away from the noise of the delivery ward and the nursery. Bring soothing music, headphones, anything that will help ease your heart even a slight bit, create a more peaceful atmosphere and take away some of the delivery ward noises you may not want to hear at this time.

- ❖ Name your child. Our hospital gave us a birth certificate and we asked them to put a label on Caleb's bassinet that told his name, weight, etc. - just like other children born in the hospital.

- ❖ Hold your baby and say hello and goodbye. Learn all that you can about them. Caleb was a BIG boy, he had

Josh's toes, my cleft chin, he looked so serious, and he had the same black curly hair as his big brother Josiah did when he was born.

- ❖ Take pictures or ask the hospital staff to take them.
- ❖ Ask the hospital staff for a lock of hair, an ink stamp or plaster imprint of handprints or footprints.
- ❖ Let other children hold the baby, as well as other family members, as long as that is alright with you and with them.
- ❖ Ask for referrals to funeral homes that are proven in doing a good job in similar situations and are sensitive to the many issues of the death of a baby.
- ❖ Start a special baby book. The funeral home provided one for us and it was very meaningful for me to fill that out, just as I filled out a baby book for Josiah, though the pages were a little different.

I hope and pray you make it through your hospital stay surrounded by people who will love you, comfort you, counsel you, console you and care for you as you struggle to make some very hard choices.

YOUR CHILD'S MEMORIAL SERVICE

God has a bottle for His people's tears. What was sown as a tear will come up as a pearl.
  ❖ *Matthew Henry*

I'd like to try and help you get through the "arrangements" of putting your child to rest here on this earth. I found that I felt numb for the first little while after Caleb's death, but I also wanted to honour him at his memorial service.

A time of honouring and remembering your baby could also be done in the privacy of your own home, no matter how tiny your baby was.

It is true - no one should ever have to bury a child. If you feel like you cannot think through the events of the next few days, please allow yourself the freedom of letting others do it for you. These are just a few suggestions that come to mind...

❖ Publish a birth/death announcement in the newspaper and keep a clipping in a special place.

❖ Ask friends or family members (including other children if that is okay with you) to sing, preach, speak at the funeral - make it as personal as possible.

❖ Allow for donations to a specific cause or charity that is important to you and your family.

❖ Choose a scripture passage that is special to you and brings you hope. We read John 14:1-4 at Caleb's funeral.

❖ Celebrate the life of your child. Tell what you **did** know about the baby, or how your life has already been impacted by them, or a funny/special story about the pregnancy/birth.

- Try to look at hope during the service.
- Some people may not be able to attend because it is too overwhelming for them, or there is too much pain involved. Try not to be upset and let everyone make their own choices about this sensitive issue. Grief looks very different in each of our lives.
- Place sentimental items in the baby's casket - things you were saving for them, or gifts from family members/friends.
- Pick songs that were special to you during your pregnancy - our choice was *I Can Only Imagine* by Mercy Me.
- Choose a meaningful inscription for your baby's tombstone if you are going to have a stone. We chose to have "Surrounded by Glory" inscribed on Caleb's tombstone (another inspiration from the song *I Can Only Imagine* - it tells of being surrounded by glory once we arrive in heaven). This inscription is a constant reminder to us of his heavenly home.

REMEMBERING YOUR CHILD AT SPECIAL OCCASIONS

Those we love never die, for as long as we live and remember, they are with us.
   ❖   *Helen Steiner Rice*

Please know that you are free to include your child as you celebrate special occasions without their presence. No matter how small they were or how short the time they were with us, they are still an important part of our lives and our families.

It may also be too hard to remember them this way – there are so many personal choices as you continue on the journey of healing. Every person will experience grief in their own way.

I'd like to share with you how we have chosen to remember Caleb at special times of the year and I encourage you to find ideas that fit with you and your family.

❖   Just before Christmas we participate in Operation Shoebox by Samaritan's Purse. Generous people ship shoeboxes full of gifts to various parts of the world so that needy children everywhere receive something for Christmas. We put together three boxes as we have three boys - our oldest and our youngest sons help to fill a box each, and we put together another one in Caleb's absence.

❖   Another Christmas tradition is to buy an ornament for each of the kids in the family, so they will have many ornaments to take with them when they leave home and put up their own tree in the future. One member of our family buys an ornament for Caleb through a worthy cause (the Memory Tree) at church. There are also Reading Trees (a book is bought for a needy child as a Christmas present in lieu of an ornament, etc.)

- ❖ For Caleb's birthday our family participates in balloon launches. We pick a beautiful spot to release a balloon and watch it soar to the heavens as we sing Happy Birthday and say a few words to Caleb if our heart desires.

- ❖ When our boys were young and it was time to have family portraits done, we would bring along a tiny, stuffed bunny that the hospital gave us when Caleb was born. One of the boys would hold it as we got our picture taken, and the bunny became part of our family portrait for a time.

- ❖ There are so many ideas out there if you search for them, or you could start your own special ways of including your child in special occasions.

HONOURING THE LIFE OF YOUR CHILD

The most beautiful things in life cannot be seen or touched. They must be felt with the heart.
   ❖ *Helen Keller*

Our babies have come and gone much too quickly through our lives, yet we will always have a memory of them, a place in our heart for them, and a love for them that is very strong. At times it was frustrating for me because I didn't know how to express my love for Caleb. He was not there to hug and kiss or experience my love for him in tangible, visible ways. Instead of trying to contain my love or minimalize it, I found other ways to show my love for Caleb and honour his life. The greatest way I accomplished this was to spread my love for Caleb around to Josh, Josiah, and Elijah - to let them in and share that special piece of my heart with them, as well as other family members, friends and other little ones in my life.

There have been many other things we have done to honour Caleb, acknowledge his memory and bless others, as we discover more and more ways God will use Caleb in this world. Some of the things we have done would never have been a thought if not for Caleb.

Here are a few ideas of how to honour your child, if you are searching for ways to express your love for them in tangible ways…

- ❖ Sponsor a needy child through World Vision or Compassion Canada.
- ❖ Plant a tree or a garden and watch it grow as you care for it (this is a great idea for helping children heal from the loss of a sibling).
- ❖ Make a donation to an organization or a project that plans to print names on bricks, plaques, etc.

- Build or purchase a memory box. Josh made a memory box with his grandfather and a good friend of ours painted beautiful pictures on it for us. I filled the box with some special items to remember Caleb.

- Discover how your local hospital cares for women who have similar experiences and contribute to their efforts.

- My devotional basket (which contains a Bible, prayer books, and a journal) is one that we received just after Caleb's death - it was originally filled with beautiful flowers.

- In lieu of starting RESPs or saving for your child's future education, consider setting up savings bonds or a trust fund that can be used by someone who cannot pay for themselves.

- The Gideons accept *In Memory Of* donations and print Bibles to hand out.

- Donate the baby items you purchased or were given specially for your baby to a pregnancy care centre or a shelter for abused women.

- Our family is looking into buying a star to celebrate 10 years of Caleb in our lives. My sister found out we can buy a star and name it – one that was discovered on Caleb's birthday. We think that will be a wonderful reminder of where Caleb lives.

FINDING PEACE

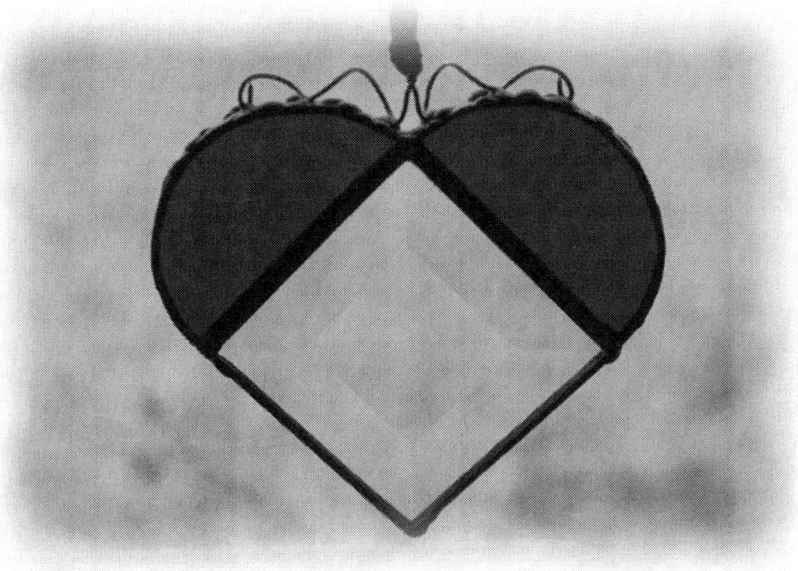

CHAPTER 16

HEAVEN

I can only imagine what it will be like, when I walk by Your side...
I can only imagine, what my eyes will see, when Your Face is before me!
I can only imagine. I can only imagine.
Surrounded by Your Glory, what will my heart feel?
Will I dance for you, Jesus? Or in awe of You, be still?
Will I stand in Your presence, or to my knees will I fall?
Will I sing 'Hallelujah!'? Will I be able to speak at all?
I can only imagine! I can only imagine!
I can only imagine, when that day comes, when I find myself standing in the Son!
I can only imagine, when all I will do, is forever, forever worship You!

❖ *I Can Only Imagine* by Mercy Me

I can tell you right now that I don't know much about heaven except that it is a place beyond imagination. It is paradise, and I am looking forward to spending my forever there with God and with those I love. The Bible doesn't give many clues as to what heaven is like. Personally, I think this is because there are no words to describe it. So, this section of the book is based primarily on personal reflections, experiences, and conversations with other people that have given me comfort these past few years.

Here are just two of the Bible verses that give us a glimpse of heaven:

Look down from heaven, your holy dwelling place.

- Deuteronomy 26:15a

(Moses advising the Israelites what to pray to God)

In my Father's house are many rooms; if it were not so, I would have told you. I am going there to prepare a place for you. And if I go and prepare a place for you, I will come back and take you to be where I am. - John 14:2-3

(Jesus talking to His disciples.)

These few words tell us that heaven is God's home, His dwelling place, and that heaven is holy. That means it is a place that is without sin or sadness. It is a perfect place. And so it has to be if God is to live there.

Also, there are many rooms in God's house, and many spots for people to come and stay awhile. Heaven is not a temporary place, it is a forever place. Jesus Himself prepared your baby's spot. Imagine your child living somewhere that Jesus has made especially for them. Jesus loves us so much that He died for us, so imagine what your baby's dwelling place would be like if the Son of God designed it. God knows all of us inside out; He knows our likes and dislikes, our favourite colours, our favourite views. The Bible says that Jesus "prepares a place for you" (John 14:2), and that means he is excited about it, anticipating the time we will meet Him there, waiting for us to join Him. We are welcome house guests of Jesus.

The most beautiful aspect of heaven is the presence of Jesus, and those who dwell in heaven experience His presence all the time. I think that must be the greatest part of living in heaven - being with Jesus.

I am simply trying to paint the tiniest part of a picture of what it must be like to live in heaven. My mind cannot grasp the beauty that must abound there.

When I was pregnant with Caleb there was a song on the radio that moved me to tears almost every time I heard it on the radio. The song *I Can Only Imagine* by Mercy Me painted such a beautiful picture of a world beyond this one.

Life was tough for us during the time Caleb was growing in my womb, and the song was a good reminder of what is to come. Of course at the time I didn't know things were about to get even tougher, and that the song would come to mean so much more for me. I believe God was preparing my heart for Caleb's death, even though the thought never crossed my mind before it actually happened.

After Caleb died, I thought about heaven all the time. Other people would tell me their thoughts on heaven and what they imagined Caleb was doing there, what it would be like to reunite with him one day, and what his heavenly home must look like. There's no possible way we can fathom an inkling of the beauty and majesty of God's dwelling place, but I think if you ask Him to give you a glimpse of your child's life as it is now in heaven, a comforting vision of your child in glory, He will reach out to you in your grief and speak to your heart like only He can.

I'd love to share with you some of the pictures of my child that I carry around in my heart, snapshots of Caleb's life in heaven...

I see my Lord and Saviour, my best friend, the one who loved me enough to die for me - I see Him rocking Caleb to sleep, I see Caleb's angelic babysitters caring for him with nothing but the characteristics of God - love, joy, peace, patience, kindness, goodness, faithfulness, gentleness, and self-control. His friends also have these same qualities and Caleb enjoys playing with them. Some of his friends may be other children who have gone on to heaven shortly before or after birth. There is only unconditional love and acceptance in all the relationships in heaven. There is no hurt or rejection, and no one is left out.

I see Caleb as a baby dancing to the music of heaven and sleeping in absolute comfort, I see him as a boy climbing the tallest trees and swimming in the bluest water, and I see him as a man talking with friends and excelling in the job he fulfills in heaven. I wonder about the colours he must see - they must be brighter and more vivid than any of the colours of our prettiest rainbows! What about the amazing people he's meeting - imagine him having conversations with Noah, Ruth, Samson, David, Esther, Daniel, etc.

Of course, you'd rather have your baby with you. There is no question of that, and I am not trying to minimize that desire - I know it well, I experience it every day. But I can think of no better place for my baby to be if not with me.

I have a special vision that always cheers me up when I miss Caleb most. When my time on earth is done and I move on to join Caleb in heaven, I just know he's going to pick me up in his arms and swing me around, and tell me he loves me and he's been waiting for me, happy and content in his heavenly home. I look forward to watching all three of my boys wrestle when we are all united in heaven. And the thought of Josh meeting another one of his sons just warms my heart every time. All in God's perfect timing.

About three years after Caleb died, I finally grabbed hold of a wonderful truth that had taken a while to sink in and really speak to my heart. I am not permanently separated from Caleb, but our meeting will be prolonged for a longer period of time than I originally thought. A normal pregnancy lasts 40 weeks, but sometimes I still feel pregnant with Caleb, in the sense that I am still waiting. It's not that I will never meet him, hold him, or hear him talk and laugh, it's just that I have to wait much longer than I thought I would. We will have a reunion one day, my son and I. How glorious it will be, there will be a lot of catching up to do. It is one of the things I look forward to at the end of my journey.

❦ CHAPTER 17 ❦

THE BRIDGE TO HEAVEN

Jesus said that those who mourn, those who are poor and persecuted and have nothing are happy! How could he say such things? Only in light of another kingdom, another world, another way of seeing this world. He came to bring life - another kind of life altogether. And it is in terms of that life that we must learn to look at our suffering. I have found it possible, when I see suffering from that perspective, wholeheartedly to accept it. But it takes a steady fixing of my gaze on the cross.
If the cross is the place where the worst thing that could happen happened, it is also the place where the best thing that could happen happened. Ultimate hatred and ultimate love met on those two crosspieces of wood. Suffering and love were brought into harmony.
 ❖ *Elisabeth Elliot*

In this book there is a real focus on the hope of heaven. I reflect on the heavenly experiences of our babies - about the joy and love they live in every day and about meeting them there one day. Heaven is the home of God. He lives there with Jesus and all those who believe in Him. There is room for everyone in heaven, regardless of background, and God wants you to spend your eternity with Him, He wants you to join Him in His heavenly home and live there with Him forever. In case you are doubtful about where you are headed for eternity, here's a short and sweet explanation of how you can be certain.

Picture with me a bridge that sits atop a wide expanse. This bridge does not meet in the middle, and the gap that exists makes it impossible to jump across. You are on one side of the bridge and God is on the other - you are separated from Him. Mistakes, wrong choices, or sin is what created the gap in the bridge. No matter how many good deeds you do, no matter how much God loves you, the gap remains. Imperfection simply cannot touch perfection. Unholiness cannot touch holiness. You just can't get to God or heaven on your own.

For all have sinned and fall short of the glory of God.- Romans 3:23

The good news is that God does not want to stay separated from you, He wants to be in relationship with you, and He has already made a way to reach you. There is someone who can repair your bridge to God, save you from falling through the middle, rescue you from your mistakes, and deliver you from an eternity that is uncertain. That someone is God's Son, Jesus Christ.

For God so loved the world that He gave His one and only Son, that whoever believes in Him should not perish but have eternal life. - John 3:16

More than two thousand years ago, Jesus Christ died on the cross for you, for me, for everyone. When Jesus went to the cross He took your sin with Him - as he died, your sin was wiped out, forgiven. And as He rose back to life He showed the world that sin, wrong choices, mistakes don't have to end in death. Jesus gave you a choice. He repaired your bridge and gave you the freedom to experience a wonderful, fulfilling relationship with God that ultimately leads to heaven. All you have to do is accept His gift of reconciliation.

All this is from God, who reconciled us to Himself through Christ and gave us the ministry of reconciliation: that God was reconciling the world to Himself in Christ, not counting men's sins against them. And He has committed to us the message of reconciliation... God made Him who had no sin to be sin for us.
- 2 Corinthians 5:18, 19, 21a

For Christ died for our sins once for all, the righteous for the unrighteous to bring you to God. - 1 Peter 3:18a

Whoever you are, whatever your past, wherever you are right now, you can take your first steps across the bridge to God and begin your journey of faith - walk, run, skip, jump, cartwheel if you want to! He started walking towards you the moment you were born. Start by talking to God. Let Him know you believe in Jesus and what He did for you at the cross. Don't worry about what words to use in your prayer, or how it may sound to God. God knows you, and all He cares about is that you mean it.

Everyone who calls on the name of the Lord [Jesus] will be saved. - Romans 10:13

That if you confess with your mouth 'Jesus is Lord,' and believe in your heart that God raised Him from the dead, you will be saved. - Romans 10:9

Turn to God, open your heart up to Him, for that is how you find your faith. Faith will help you believe and know the love of God and His Son, Jesus. Then you can be certain that you will spend your forever in heaven, with God and with your baby.

This is only the beginning of your faith journey. I can tell you from personal experience that being in relationship with God is the best thing I've done with my life. I learn more about Him by reading the Bible, praying, and spending time with other christians. My heavenly Father is my best friend - He is there with me through good times and bad, heartache and joy, triumph and sorrow. He has always been with me, patiently waiting until I was ready to believe in Him, know Him, and share my life with Him. He is the greatest companion on the journey of faith and on the journey of healing.

THERE IS HOPE

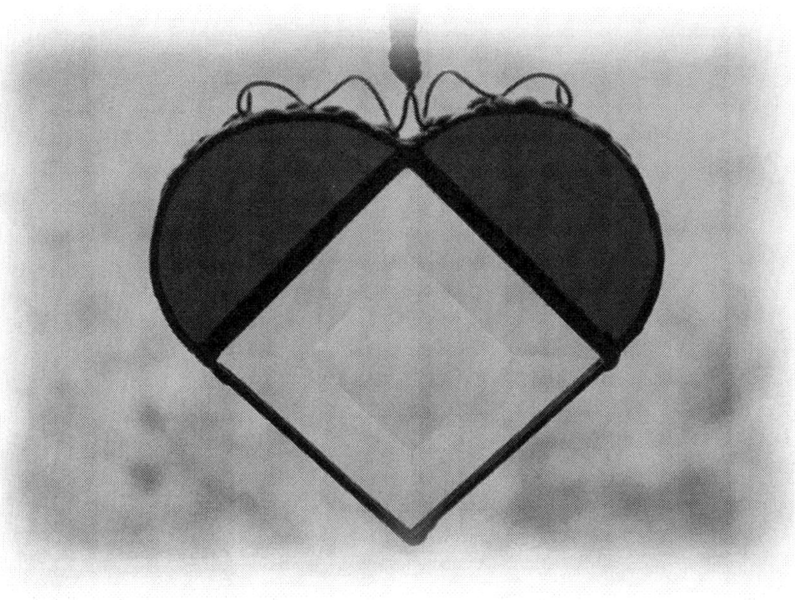

CHAPTER 18
WHAT ABOUT MY PLANS

For I know the plans I have for you, declares the Lord, plans to prosper you and not to harm you, plans to give you hope and a future.

❖ *Jeremiah 29:11*

So... what about Caleb's hope and future? I can tell you right now that my middle son's hope and future are not what I thought they would be. He was supposed to fill our days with many wonderful memories for decades to come. He was supposed to play with his older brother, splash in the bath, run through the puddles in cute rubber boots, and I was supposed to have an abundance of tickle fights with him. I was supposed to read him lots of stories from his Baby Bible, and teach him Jesus Loves Me. I was supposed to be there as he took his first steps, experienced his first day of school, played sports, married the woman of his dreams and became a parent himself. These were all the things I hoped for Caleb's future. Why didn't it happen this way? The hard truth is that I will never understand.

When Caleb passed, people would tell me how God's purposes for his life had already been fulfilled, and his time on this earth, though incredibly short, was done. One of the hardest things I had to deal with was giving over what I had intended Caleb to be in my life, Josh's life, Josiah's life, Elijah's life, and the lives of our family members.

I'm sorry I don't have the answers that I know you are looking for. Those answers wait in a place far beyond this one. One day it will all make perfect sense, though I know that sometimes that doesn't seem good enough.

For now, I hold onto this thought: God has His perfect plans for us all, and God's plans for Caleb are being fulfilled, though they are vastly different from my plans. The hard part is opening myself up to what God intended Caleb to be, to open my heart and see through God's eyes to what Caleb has done instead of what he hasn't done. I have a responsibility to search for God's plans for Caleb, just as I do for my other two boys. I will be getting to know Caleb all my life as God unfolds to me what he is in our lives, instead of what he was supposed to be. Caleb's time on earth was much shorter than I ever imagined, but his life can still be all that God intends, and I can help in that by opening myself up to His purposes for my tiny boy.

About six weeks after Caleb's death I started making a list. This list helped me focus on God's purposes and plans for Caleb instead of constantly thinking about the unfairness of his death.

These are some of the highlights from my special list…

- ❖ There were people at Caleb's funeral who never go to church or go to a church where they cannot hear the gospel – **they heard the gospel on May 23rd, 2003.**

- ❖ Many women have opened up to me about their own loss of a child. Caleb's funeral brought closure and healing in many women's lives and also a chance to just remember their own babies and know they are safe in heaven and are cared for by Jesus and they **will** see them one day or see them again.

- ❖ A woman shared with me that she had a very similar experience to ours, and they actually buried their son on the exact same date as we buried Caleb, 16 years earlier.

- A woman shared with me she lost twins at 7 months in utero from abuse from her husband. I gave her one of my The Gift plaques and she hung it where she can see it every day as she sews.
- Josh shared Caleb's story with the staff at camp.
- As far as I can tell - so many family and friends are thinking about heaven now, feeling like a piece of them is already there. Caleb has brought them closer to God and reminded us all of the glory of heaven.
- Josh shared Caleb's story again at camp - this time with the whole camp - about 30 people.
- Found out that a good friend just lost her daughter - very similar circumstances. I was able to truly reach out to her in her grief and loss, though just through email. She has shared and I have shared - beautiful connecting moments. I have been able to pray with tears and depth for her, truly intercessory, feel her pain and come before God on her behalf.
- Seen a real depth to many family members that I've never seen before. They are also adopting some of their own special ways to remember Caleb - a Christmas ornament on the memory tree at church every year, balloon launches of their own on his birthday - their souls have truly touched and loved and grieved my son.

CHAPTER 19
WHAT ABOUT MY FAITH

REACH OUT TO GOD INSTEAD OF TURNING FROM HIM

Stand still and whisper God's name, and listen. He is nearer than you think.
❖ *Max Lucado*

When Caleb died, I don't remember feeling much anger, just a lot of confusion. I lived my life in such a daze for a long time, feeling so lost, not understanding the death of my baby or the reasons for it. I was confused about this God I had vowed to love and serve for the rest of my life. There were so many questions I needed to be answered, so much pain to deal with, and my whole view of Christianity, God and faith was shaken to the core.

I had a choice in my initial grief - to reach out to God and allow Him to help me heal, or to turn from Him in my confusion and pain. Though I did not understand the loss, I could understand that my Heavenly Father wanted to comfort me. I knew that He loved me, in spite of any negative feelings I had toward Him at the time.

For you created my inmost being; you knit me together in my mother's womb. - Psalm 139:13

Be honest with God about whatever emotions you are having. He made you who you are, He knew every second of your life before time began, He knows you better than anyone else, He knows all your thoughts and feelings, and He can handle every single one of them. Talk to Him, question Him, yell at Him, but don't turn away from Him. Don't abandon your faith; it is the one thing that will carry you through your grief.

I wrote these words for a newsletter in May 2008...

Blessed are those who mourn, for they will be comforted.
- Matthew 5:4

*We have all experienced sadness or grief in our lives - whether it's losing a friend or family member, or living with unrealized dreams and ambitions, or regretting decisions and experiences from our past. Life certainly isn't easy and hard times are inevitable. It is normal to mourn, but there is hope for us in this verse. There is a promise from Almighty God, and He **cannot** break a promise. God doesn't say we will understand. He doesn't say we will never be angry and confused. He simply says we will be comforted.*
*What has that comfort looked like in your life? It might be hard to see, you might have to search for it. It might be hidden in a special card, the chorus of a song, a conversation with a friend, or a passage of scripture. When our middle son was stillborn five years ago, I found comfort in the passing of time - each day was easier than the last. God gives us His promise, He can be trusted, and you **will** find comfort.*

At Caleb's funeral a woman said something extremely impacting to me. She reminded me that God had also experienced the death of a child - His Son, Jesus. I knew she was right, but it took me a while to process this thought and let it settle in my heart. The circumstances of Christ's death were very different, but the truth in her words has stayed with me these past few years. God knows my grief, He knows your grief, and He understands what it's like to have a child die way before their time.

And a voice from heaven said, "This is my Son, whom I love; with Him I am well pleased." - Matthew 3:17

There is no doubt God loves His Son. How much more intense is the grief of God in knowing He could have stopped Jesus' death at any moment? I cannot possibly comprehend the implications of that truth.

And surely I am with you always, to the very end of the age.
- Matthew 28:20b

Your Heavenly Father will help you along as you reach out to Him. It's not all up to you; He'll meet you where you're at. There is no doubt that He will find a way to show you His love, He knows what speaks to your heart.

He heals the broken-hearted and binds up their wounds
- Psalm 147:3

Even though I walk through the valley of the shadow of death, I will fear no evil, for you are with me; your rod and your staff, they comfort me. - Psalm 23:4

The only thing you have to do is be open to seeing it. That might take time and we all move at a different pace. He knows that, and He'll wait. He really does love you, and loves your child as well, more than you can imagine. I'm sorry for your pain, I know it well, and though I will never understand why any of us have to endure the loss, I do understand that God does not leave us alone on the journey of healing. I will continue on the path God has laid out for me, trying my best to seek His face with whatever comes, reaching out to Him instead of turning from Him.

TRUST

Trust in the Lord with all your heart and lean not on your own understanding. - Proverbs 3:5

  Caleb taught me to live out a whole new level of trust. Something deeper than anything else. God is always asking us to trust Him, and sometimes I have trouble even in the small things, so I found it so hard and confusing to trust Him with something this big - the life of my child. I had all these hopes and dreams for Caleb - none of them will be realized. Aren't children in our lives so we can care for them and be responsible for them? Then why isn't Caleb here with me? Again, I do not understand. I've had to let go of so many of the questions that were eating me up inside in order to continue on my journey of healing.

The Lord is a refuge for the oppressed, a stronghold in times of trouble. Those who know Your name will trust in You, for You, Lord, have never forsaken those who seek You. - Psalm 9:9-10

  There is a promise in this verse that we will trust God. I have no doubt He will help us to trust Him as we walk this journey. Our job is to make the conscious choice to trust... not an easy one in the least. I don't know how many times I heard this gentle whisper of God's voice in my soul, asking me to trust Him. Some days it was impossible, but the whisper remained, I knew there was great love and comfort waiting for me in the choice to trust. Time was a great healer for me and over time I realized I didn't have to agree with or understand Caleb's death, I just had to trust God and leave it in His big, strong, capable hands.

The Lord is my strength and my shield; my heart trusts in Him, and I am helped. My heart leaps for joy and I will give thanks to Him in song. - Psalm 28:7

*I know there are times
your dreams turn to dust
you wonder as you cry
why it has to hurt so much
give Me all your sadness
someday you will know the reason why
with a child-like heart
simply put your hope in Me*

*Take My hand and walk where I lead
keep your eyes on Me alone
don't you say why were
the old days better
just because you're
scared of the unknown
take My hand and walk*

*Don't live in the past
cause yesterday's gone
wishing memories would last
you're afraid to carry on
you don't know what's comin'
but you know the one who holds tomorrow
I will be your guide
take you through the night
if you keep your eyes on Me
Just like a child
holdings daddy's hand
don't let go of mine
you know you can't stand
on your own*

❖ *Take My Hand* **by The Kry**

KEEPING IT REAL

Though we know God is not to blame for any death, so many times it seems that He turns a blind eye by allowing His permissive will to occur. He stands dead-centre when we are looking for a target. I'm convinced that God loves us so much that He is willing to take the blame, to absorb our anger when we need a punching bag. I think He would rather have us yelling at Him than not speaking at all.

❖ Leslie Williams

It's a hard shake of reality to lose a child. The world is sometimes such a broken, ugly place full of the most painful experiences and emotions. Being a Christian doesn't always shield us from the hurt, but our faith definitely helps us persevere.

Following Christ, being a Christian, doesn't mean you have to have a smile plastered on your face no matter what, and it doesn't mean you don't feel things deeply. Christ was never afraid to let others know about his feelings. He experienced some of the deepest human feelings during his 33 years of life...

- ❖ Jesus experienced great anger in the temple when he discovered people were treating it as a marketplace (Matthew 21:12-13, Mark 11:15-17)
- ❖ Jesus experienced great sadness as he wept for Jerusalem and the hardships he knew were coming for the people of the city (Mathew 23:37-39, Luke 13:34-35)
- ❖ Jesus experienced great sorrow when his friend Lazarus died (John 11:32-36)
- ❖ Jesus experienced a great struggle with following the will of God just before his arrest (Matthew 26:36-46)

Don't be afraid to come to God with your deepest feelings. He knows them well. He can handle them all.

A good friend of mine wrote these words for a newsletter in October 2008...

Do you ever get the impression that Christians are supposed to be happy all the time, but wonder what's wrong with you because you know that when reality hits, you're not smiling all the time? Well I truly believe that the "Happy Christian" is really a myth... Christians aren't obligated to be smiling all the time... if we are, we aren't truly being real.

The problem is that people use two very different words interchangeably: joy and happiness.

Happiness is circumstantial. We all experience happy moments: our wedding day, the birth of a child, their first steps or graduation, promotions at work, dream-like vacations, or even the day to day reminders that life is good... the sweet words of a loved one, relaxing outside under a perfect blue sky... you can make a mental list of those moments that have brought you happiness. Unfortunately they don't last forever. We cannot escape times of sadness, disappointment and deep pain. They are a reality in all of our lives. Ecclesiastes 3:4 assures us that there is "a time to weep and a time to laugh."

Now for that second word: joy. What makes it different? In short, joy defies its circumstances. It is to be noted that joy is a fruit of the Spirit (Galatians 5:22-23) which we possess once we accept Christ as our Saviour. In essence, happiness is a response to externals, whereas true joy is a response to what's inside... the security in our salvation through Christ and the peace of knowing that God is active in our daily lives. Even though I may be facing uncertainty, exhaustion, discouragement or sadness, deep down knowing that I have a God who is bigger than my circumstances, a

God who loves me and is powerful enough to carry me through gives me peace, hope, and ultimately joy. I often find myself recalling Philippians 4:6.

Fleeting moments of happiness may come at various points in our lives, but inner joy flows only from Christ. Times of sorrow will come... but seek Him to get you through, as He is our joy. The following verses remind us that God never leaves us despite the tough days... May they give you a taste of joy regardless of what you may be facing...

Isaiah 40:25-31
Isaiah 41:10
Isaiah 49:13
Psalm 103:2-5
Jeremiah 29:11-14
Jeremiah 32:17

❖ *Melanie Heffern*

Death is nothing at all. I have only slipped away into the next room. I am I, and you are you. Whatever we were to each other, that we still are. Call me by my old familiar name, speak to me in the easy way which we always used. Put no difference in your tone, wear no forced air of solemnity or sorrow. Laugh as we always laughed at the little jokes we enjoyed together. Let my name be ever the household word that is always was, let it be spoken without effect, without the trace of a shadow on it. Life means all that it ever meant. It is the same as it ever was; there is unbroken continuity. Why should I be out of mind because I am out of sight? I am waiting for you, for an interval, somewhere very near, just round the corner. All is well.

Henry Scott Holland

1847-1918

Canon of St. Paul's Cathedral

WORDS FOR THE JOURNEY

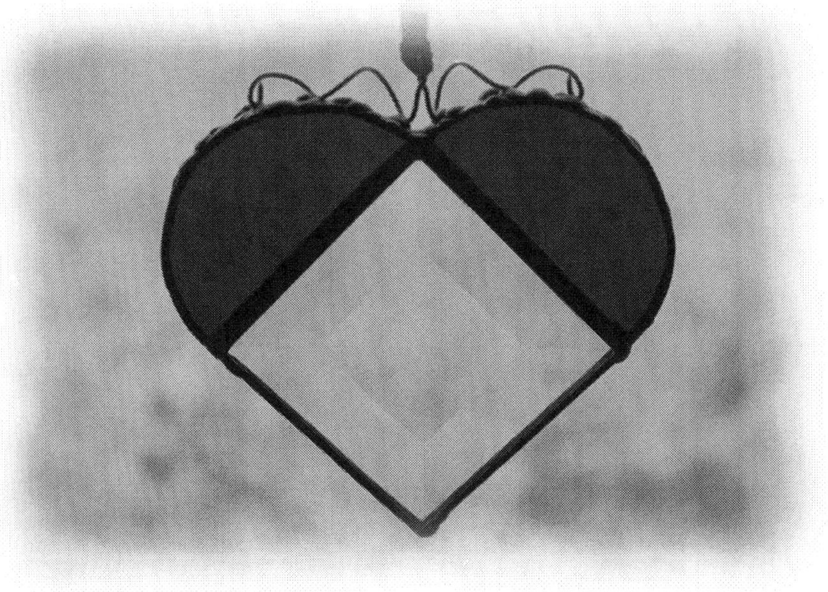

CHAPTER 19
FAREWELL FOR NOW...

We can cry with hope
We can say goodbye with hope
'Cause we know our goodbye is not the end, oh no
And we can grieve with hope
'Cause we believe with hope
(There's a place by God's grace)
There's a place where we'll see your face again
We'll see your face again
❖ *With Hope,* Steven Curtis Chapman

Since the idea of this book began in my heart in early 2004, I have heard of many more instances of pregnancy or newborn loss. I have been able to reach out to some, and pray for others. I have connected with many women who have experienced the loss of a baby, and I've been able to share my story many times, in hopes that it would help in some way. You are not alone in your grief, I am not alone in mine, and I will always wish that none of us had to endure this loss. But I am glad for companions on the journey, I am glad to walk with you for a while on your journey, and I hope others will gather around you as you travel one step at a time towards healing.

The best companion for the journey is Jesus - He will always be there, reaching out His hand to you, always patient, always helping you along. Even when you don't want His help, when you just want to trail behind on the journey, feeling lost and alone, He's still there - waiting.

Thank you for letting me share the journey of healing with you. May God's peace fall heavy upon you as you navigate the path of grief. May God's comfort ease the pain. And may God's love light your way clear.

May I invite my husband to walk with you for a few moments?

These are some wonderful words that Josh wrote five years after Caleb's death...

I was not sure how long it would take for my life to return to "normal." I had been ready for my life to have a new definition of normal with the addition of a second son; now it was to be a different normal than I had expected, one without Caleb Joshua Freedom. It took me a while to understand that when a huge thing like this happens in life, we must redefine normal.

Five years from the death of Caleb and of many of my dreams, I have a new normal, and my life goes on. That does not mean that I don't long for the old and anticipated normal. But I do want my new normal not to be overwhelmed by the old normal, so I keep moving ahead. That does not change the fact that there have been times in my life this past five years where there has been a profound sense of something missing. Tonight I put my two sons, Josiah and Elijah, to bed in our camper. I tucked them in side by side and the thought burst on me unheeded that I should be tucking in three, not two. I still am a wreck when we visit the grave site and I don't know if I will ever stop being a wreck. I don't think that I want to, truth being told.

The hardest thing that I went through was the creation of the new normal. But I found reasons to keep going. Mine were different from yours, but find them. These words I write now are out of my experience and though they seem painful, they are not intended to hurt. The loss of a child changed me, created a new normal, and cut me deeply. But I worked through the pain, acknowledged the grief, and found that God gave the strength to move ahead. And in the midst of moving ahead, I have learned to celebrate that which I have, not that which I have lost.

This is what I know for sure; these things that I know I have:

I have a wife of grace and beauty and wisdom who carries me even as I carry her.

I have three beautiful sons, who each bring joy to my heart in different ways.

I have two sons here who need me to live life to the fullest.

I have the anticipation of meeting Caleb one day, and what a day it shall be.

I have a just and merciful God who cares for me, for my family, and always will.

I have all that I need, and petty concerns fade more and more as I remember the things I do have, not what I have lost.

The way through this pain was to just keep going... keep journeying through the grief and keep discovering hope.

❖ *Josh Sklar*

SCRIPTURE TO COMFORT YOU

Psalm 6:6 - *I am worn out from groaning; all night long I flood my bed with weeping and drench my couch with tears.*

Psalm 23:1-4 -*The Lord is my shepherd, I shall lack nothing. He makes me lie down in green pastures, He leads me beside quiet waters, He restores my soul. He guides me in paths of righteousness for His name's sake. Even though I walk through the valley of the shadow of death, I will fear no evil, for You are with me; Your rod and staff, they comfort me.*

Psalm 29:11 - *The Lord gives strength to His people; the Lord blesses His people with peace.*

Psalm 31:24 - *Be strong and take heart, all you who hope in the Lord.*

Psalm 42:11 – *Why are you so downcast, O my soul? Why so disturbed within me? Put your hope in God, for I will yet praise Him, my Saviour and my God.*

Psalm 46:10a - *Be still and know that I am God.*

Psalm 84:10a – *Better is one day in your courts than a thousand elsewhere.*

Psalm 119:50 – *Remember your word to your servant, for you have given me hope. My comfort in my suffering is this: your promise preserves my life.*

Isaiah 25:8a - *He will swallow up death forever. The Sovereign Lord will wipe away the tears from all faces...*

Isaiah 41:13 *-For I am the Lord, your God, who takes hold of your right hand and says to you, Do not fear; I will help you.*

Isaiah 53:4-5 - *Surely [Jesus] took up our infirmities and carried our sorrows, yet we considered Him stricken by God, smitten by Him, and afflicted. But He was pierced for our transgressions, He was crushed for our iniquities; the punishment that brought us peace was upon Him, and by His wounds we are healed.*

Isaiah 65:20a - *Never again will there be in it an infant that lives but a few days...(Speaking about the new earth)*

Romans 8:26 – *In the same way, the Spirit helps us in our weakness. We do not know what we ought to pray for, but the Spirit himself intercedes for us with groans that words cannot express.*

Romans 8:35&37 - *Who shall separate us from the love of Christ? Shall trouble or hardship or persecution or famine or nakedness or danger or sword? No, in all these we are more than conquerors through Him who loved us.*

Revelation 21:4 - *He will wipe every tear from their eyes. There will be no more death or mourning or crying or pain, for the old order of things has passed away.*

BOOKS TO HELP YOU HEAL

These books are recommended by myself or other trusted sources...

Grieving the Child I Never Knew
- Kathe Winnenberg
This is a wonderful devotional that helped me in my journey.

Forever Silent and Forever Changed: The Loss of a Baby in Miscarriage, Stillbirth, Early Infancy. A Mother's Experience and Your Personal Journal
- Kellie Davis

A Rose in Heaven - A Journey of Hope and Healing For Those Who Have Lost a Baby
- Dawn Siegrest Waltman

Empty Arms: Coping with Miscarriage, Stillbirth and Infant Death
- Sherokee Ilse

Empty Cradle, Broken Heart: Surviving the Death of Your Baby
- Deborah Davis

Empty Arms: Emotional Support for Those Who Have Suffered Miscarriage or Stillbirth
- Pam Vredvelt

The Ache for a Child
- Debra Bridwell
- Pregnancy loss and infertility.

Forever Our Angels
- Hannah Stone
- Personal stories of miscarriage told by men and women.

Remembering Our Angels
- Hannah Stone
- Personal stories of miscarriage told by men and women.

Life Touches Life: A Mother's Story of Stillbirth and Healing
- Lorraine Ash

Tender Fingerprints
- Brad Stetson
- A father's story of his son's stillbirth and his own struggle with grief and God.

A Guide For Fathers: When A Baby Dies
- Tim Nelson

For Better or Worse: For Couples Whose Child Has Died
- Maribeth Wilder Doerr
- Helps couples understand the grief process after losing a child, how grief affects their marriage and how to nurture the marriage. Focus is on loss due to miscarriage, stillbirth or neonatal death.

Forgotten Tears: A Grandmother's Journey Through Grief
- Nina Bennett

Safe in the Arms of God - Truth From Heaven About the Death of a Child
- John McArthur

Heaven
- Joni Erickson Tada

Grief Unseen: Healing Pregnancy Loss Through the Arts
- Laura Seftel

A Grief Observed
- C.S. Lewis

The God of All Comfort
- Hannah Whitall Smith

When Bad Things Happen to Good People
- Harold S. Kushner

Where is God When it Hurts?
- Philip Yancey

When God Doesn't Make Sense
- Dr. James Dobson

Deeper Than Tears - Promises of Comfort and Hope
- Countryman, 2001

How Big Is Your Umbrella?
- Sheila Wray Gregoire

Children's Books

Mommy Please Don't Cry
- Lynda DeYmaz

We Were Gonna Have a Baby, But We Had an Angel Instead
- Pat Schwiebert

Thumpy's Story: A Story of Love & Grief Shared by Thumpy the Bunny
- Nancy Dodge

Heaven's Brightest Star
- Kara M. Glad

Get Sad When Someone Dies
- Timothy Shinada-Izotov
- Written by a 6-year-old boy and illustrated by his mother

Help Me Say Goodbye: Activities For Helping Kids Cope When a Special Person Dies
- Silverman

Lifetimes
-Bryan Mellonie

WEBSITES AND ORGANIZATIONS FOR YOU TO VISIT

March of Dimes
Many helpful web pages about Pregnancy and Newborn Loss
http://www.marchofdimes.com/pnhec/572.asp

Caleb Cares
Prayer, scripture, stories of other grieving parents, and treasure boxes full of keepsake items and resources
www.calebministries.org

Mommies Enduring Neonatal Death
Online forums, newsletters, family memorial web pages, resources, links, keepsake items, and music
www.mend.org

Sufficient Grace Ministries
"Comforting others with the comfort we have received"
Keepsake items, newsletters and a wonderful blog
www.sufficientgrace.net
http://blog.sufficientgraceministries.org/

SHARE - Pregnancy and Infant Loss, Inc.
http://www.nationalshare.org/

Center for Loss in Multiple Births (CLIMB), Inc.
www.climb-support.org

The Compassionate Friends
"Supporting family after a child dies"
www.compassionatefriends.org

The Hope Monument
"Sculptures of all sizes to remember our babies"
Some have also created healing Gardens of Hope that feature a sculpture
www.hopemonument.com

A Place to Remember
Support materials, resources, greeting cards and keepsake items (including a memory box)
www.aplacetoremember.com

Centering Corporation - Your Grief Resource Center
Resources, magazine, cards, and journals
www.centering.org

Silent Grief
"A message of hope for the grieving heart"
Articles, chat boards and resources
www.silentgrief.com

Babies Remembered
"Your grieving, healing, and helping needs all in one place"
Guidance for families and care providers, resources, ezines, eShop, and much more
http://babiesremembered.org/

MUSIC TO SOOTHE YOUR SOUL

I Can Only Imagine - Mercy Me

Take My Hand - The Kry

Cry Out to Jesus – Third Day

Held - Natalie Grant

It is Well With My Soul - Horatio Spafford

His Eye is on the Sparrow - Civilla D. Martin

Blessed Be Your Name - Matt Redman

God I Need You Now – Plumb

My Name — George Canyon

Heaven is the Place – Steven Curtis Chapman

With Hope - Steven Curtis Chapman

 - This popular Christian singer had an adopted daughter who died on the 5th anniversary of our Caleb's birthday, so this tragedy has a special place in my heart, and I'm so glad Steven Chapman gave us a song that reminds us of the hope we have, even in times of suffering and loss.

POEMS TO TOUCH YOUR HEART

There is a Perfect Father

There is a perfect father
He never stops loving
He never stops giving
He never stops caring.
We are in His hands.

There is a perfect father
He blesses those who mourn
He comforts those in sorrow
He binds up the brokenhearted.
We are in His hands.

There is a perfect father
He reaches out to children
He blesses them and holds them
He draws them to Himself
We are in His hands.

There is a perfect father
He carries our son
He holds him until we can
He will never fail our boy
We are with Caleb, in His hands.

❖ *Josh Sklar*

God Help Me

God help me.
They say not to blame me.
They say nothing I did could have saved the baby.
God help me.
For my other children, I try to be happy.
Seeing my tears, I can't have them feel any agony.
God help me.
I'm trying not to constantly think that my two should be three,
Trying to be content, thankful with what God has given me.
God help me.
I'm trying not to obsess what my baby would be,
Boy or girl, it didn't matter to me.
God help me.
They say nothing I did could have saved the baby,
How could that be? It was inside my own body.
God help me.

❖ *Amanda Woodward*

Have Hope

Have hope.
In this painful
lonely time,
Embrace the love in your life.
Cherish the memories.
Honor the life.
Have hope.

Say goodbye.
Remember!
Release when you can.
Yet, hold one
To the love
And the dreams.
Be the parent.
Always.
Have hope.

Grieve.
Face the struggle.
Share your feelings.
Seek support.
Express the pain
And the love.
Have hope.

Take control.
Be an advocate.
Let go of that which
You cannot control.
Speak up.
Tell others.
Take hope.

Look ahead.
Dream new dreams.
Make new plans.
Find your 'new normal'

Yet, remember,
As you go forward,
Changed in many ways.

Take hope.
Believe.
Believe in yourself.
Believe in your partner.
Believe in your faith.
Believe in new dreams.
Believe in hope.
Take hope.

❖ *Sherokee Ilse, 1995 - Poem used with permission*

Sherokee is a bereaved parent, author of **Empty Arms** *and 16 other books, professional bereavement trainer, and parent advocate*
www.BabiesRemembered.org

Forget Me Not

Our little ones whisper,
"Forget me not,"
As their specialness wraps
Around our aching hearts.

Their short little lives
Hold meaning and love.
Their spirits have touched us -
Each and everyone.

They have left their gifts
For us to uncover,
If we open our eyes,
Our hearts, and our minds.

The road to discovery
Is hilly, deep, and dark.
Will we long harbor only the pain
Or set our wings for the light?

Our lives have been changed,
Our paths filled with sorrow.
Yet, their memories embrace us,
And our love lasts forever.

If we open our hearts,
Their gifts shall unfold,
As we
Forget them not!

❖ *Sherokee Ilse, 1993 - Poem used with permission*

In The Arms of Jesus

Daddy please don't look so sad,
Mommy please don't cry,
Cause I'm in the arms of Jesus and
He sings me lullabies.
Please try not to question God,
Don't think He is unkind.
Don't think He sent me to you,
And then He changed His mind.
You see, I am a special child,
And I'm needed up above,
I'm the special gift you gave Him,
The product of your love.
I'll always be there with you,
And watch the sky at night
Find the brightest star that's gleaming,
That's my halo's brilliant light.
You'll see me in the morning frost,
That mists your windowpane.
That's me, in the summer showers,
I'll be dancing in the rain.
When you feel a gentle breeze,
From a gentle wind that blows,
That's me, I'll be there,
Planting a kiss on your nose.
When you see a child playing,
And your heart feels a little tug,
That's me, I'll be there,
giving your heart a hug.
So daddy please don't look so sad,
Mommy please don't cry.
I'm in the arms of Jesus and
He sings me lullabies.

❖ *Claudette T. Allen*

My Precious Little Baby

My Precious Little Baby,
Your face I've never seen.
Your skin I've never touched before,
Nor held you close to me.
You lived inside my body,
But only for a while;
Till Jesus softly whispered,
"Come home my little child."
You must have been a special child;
If God needed you up there.
Because heaven is a better home,
Its beauty can't compare.
So, 'til I get to heaven,
And see your shining face;
Jesus will take care of you,
And love you in my place.
Yes, Jesus loves His little lambs,
They sit around His throne;
So sit on Jesus' lap dear child--
'Til Mommy gets called home.

❖ *Author Unknown*

Keep sharing the journey of healing…

Find us on Facebook:
https://www.facebook.com/discoveringhopeannasklar

We'll keep posting new resources, blog posts, poems, stories, music and more.

Or visit Anna's blog – Living in the Moments:
http://annasklar.wordpress.com

We'll keep discovering hope…

Together

Anna has been writing ever since she can remember. It is the best way she can make sense of this life. She's tried it all – poems, short stories, children's stories, articles, essays, newsletters, blog posts, and now a book.

This book was written as Anna journeyed through the first ten years of healing after the stillbirth of her middle son, Caleb Joshua Freedom Sklar, on May 21, 2003.

Anna lives with her husband and two sons in Northern Ontario. She recently received a Bachelor in Liberal Arts (with a minor in International Studies) after 21 years of chipping away at the degree. Anna loves to volunteer at church, school, and camp. She is married to a minister/church-planter/rugby professor. The two sons she is raising fill her life with blessings, even on the hard days.

Find more of Anna's writings on her blog:
Living in the Moments – http://annasklar.wordpress.com.

Made in the USA
Charleston, SC
03 October 2015